C0-AVN-490

VISIONS FOR THE 21ST CENTURY

VISIONS FOR THE 21ST CENTURY

Edited by Sheila M. Moorcroft

PRAEGER

Westport, Connecticut

0490097̶2̶   1̶7̶5̶3̶8̶3̶

Published in the United States and Canada by
Praeger Publishers, 88 Post Road West, Westport, CT 06881,
an imprint of Greenwood Publishing Group, Inc.

English language edition, except the United States and Canada,
published by Adamantine Press, England

First published 1993

Library of Congress Cataloging-in-Publication Data

Visions for the 21st century/edited by Sheila M. Moorcroft.
    p.   cm.
    Includes bibliographical references (p.   ) and index.
    ISBN 0–275–94571–5 (hc: alk. paper).—ISBN 0–275–94572–3 (pb: alk. paper)
    1. Twenty-first century—Forecasts.   I. Moorcroft, Sheila.
II. Title: Visions for the twenty-first century.
CB161.V59   1993
303.48′2′0905—dc20   92–35824
                CIP

Copyright © 1993 by Adamantine Press Ltd

All Rights Reserved. No part of this publication may be reproduced,
stored in a retrieval system or transmitted in any form or by any
means: electronic, electrostatic, magnetic tape, mechanical, photocopying,
recording or otherwise, without permission in writing from the publishers.

Library of Congress Catalog Card Number: 92–35824

ISBN: 0–275–94572–3 (pb)   0–275–94571–5 (hc)

Printed in Great Britain

TO ALL OUR FUTURES

CONTENTS

175963

0490972

PREFACE

Visions, dreams, hopes, ambition, goals, objectives, plans – we all think about the future in one way or another. And yet, and yet . . . how little time we take to ponder the potential of that future, to unravel the complexities of the here and now to enable us to see beyond the pressures of today. All too often, it is the enormity of the problems that we have fixed in our gaze, while we trample unawares on the seeds of hope, the new shoots burgeoning and bursting all around us.

In this book we do not presume to foretell what cannot be foretold, nor to prescribe what should not be prescribed. You will not find grand schemes, ready made solutions or complete pictures of the future. Rather, we hope to inspire, challenge and empower you to think about what could be, what future you would like to see; to see that each and every one of us can contribute to that future, and that it is indeed our shared responsibility; to realise that the future is not ours and ours alone to do with as we wish, but our children's and their children's for generations to come. We are simply the temporary keepers of the door.

But where to start?

As with any journey, we must start from where we are today, then think about where we would like to go. Once those essential points of reference are established, the possible routes, means of transport and supplies needed along the way, the likely obstacles and pitfalls of the various routes, not to mention their benefits and attractions, become relatively straightforward. Getting there is ultimately not the problem: it is knowing where we want to go.

In thinking about where we are and where we might want to go, we have deliberately brought together contributions which span the globe in terms of their cultural origins. The range of academic perspective is, purposefully, equally varied. No single discipline, culture or group can hope to unravel the complexity of the issues that face us. Just as the issues are inseparably interrelated, so we must begin to look for solutions and perspectives which begin to reflect and accept that interconnectedness.

Several contributions help us see what is happening now, and where that might lead in the economy, scientific method and cultural identity. Others highlight the priorities and issues which we need to address on a global scale if we are to have any hope of fulfilling our responsibility to future generations – peace, the environment and democracy. We as individuals and business as a collective body with the wherewithal to act effectively are shown to be the guardians of the future. Technology and new priorities provide the solution.

The advent of a new millennium is a rare and special time. It provides a sense of perspective, a 'timemark' on the horizon, a new beginning. We are also witnessing the flowering of the first mass movement of the future: the fight to save the environment. What better time to stop and think a while, to try and hear a still small voice of quiet in the hubbub of today.

Sheila Moorcroft
Editor, Visions for the 21st Century

THE GREAT BALANCING ACT

James B. Smith

Up on a tightrope
High upon that wire
Now can seem forever
Between reason and desire

'Beware the shifting winds
That topple both rigid and weak
Death will claim us all in time
Its way we need not seek'

Though such advice is welcomed
Where sidesteps seem worse than none
A wider path awaits him
Whose head and heart are one

Visions of a new world order can come and go, but people must carry on between dreams.

As the 21st century approaches, shoppers for a better vision of tomorrow will find no lack of vendors. Boutiques sit side by side with retail giants, each employing sophisticated communications technology to market the pathway to futures with titles such as:

'Transformation of Consciousness'

'Sustainable Environment,'

'Global Marketplace'

As a shopper, myself, I admit I am attracted to each of these visions. Together they offer a spiritual wholeness, appreciation of nature, and personal freedom – that appeals to me.

But I have some reason to believe I am not alone in this feeling. For several years, I have had the pleasure of working with a number of good people who think about the future. (Some of these individuals – including Jay Ogilvy, Willis Harman, and Geoffrey Woodling – share some of their thoughts elsewhere in this book.) Part of this work has been to examine a stream of so-called 'early signals or potential 'change' and to look for patterns in the stream that may be indicative of issues that could emerge in the future.

For example, in the latter part of the 1970s, a variety of seemingly unconnected signals suggested a fundamental change in values in the United States. I believe that shift – which at the time I dubbed 'the return of the hard-line society' – supported an event few thought likely at the time: the election of Ronald Reagan as President of the United States.

Coming back to the three visions above, the one with which I am most familiar is the 'global marketplace' (a future described by Ogilvy and others at the Global Business Network). I believe a case can be made for this vision in which the myriad of transactions in the global marketplace slowly but surely brings social and material benefit to a larger and larger share of mankind.

What makes me a bit uncomfortable with this vision of the future is that some of the signals we have been detecting suggest that new scarcities are emerging which are not adequately accounted for in this 'global marketplace' vision of the future. One of these new scarcities is 'meaning' – which will hardly be a revelation for those who envision a transformation of consciousness or even environmental sustainability.

For one reason or another, many lives which have become relatively comfortable materially seem to remain spiritually impoverished, resulting in a sense of futility captured beautifully years ago by singer Peggy Lee in her song, 'Is That All There Is?' If this scarcity exists and is spreading, what explains it? Perhaps, it is simply a natural by-product of the change from the modern era, with its foundations in science, to the postmodern era embracing acceptance of a range of realities and sources of 'truth.'

Though I am not as familiar with the other two visions of the future described above, I suspect each has potential weaknesses known to those who have pursued them for some time. But this does not matter. Barring a spiritual, ecological, material, or political upheaval of major proportions, I see no reason to expect that the new world order of the 21st century will be anything but the disorderly competition among the type of (holistic) visions set forth above.

What is more important is the degree to which individuals – and those who affect their choices – work to create wider paths to the alternate visions they may wish to pursue. Creating this infrastructure will require investments in health, education, economic growth, human rights, and other tools. Hopeful signals that suggest such investment will be well under way by the close of this century make me optimistic about the beginning of the next one.

THE FUTURE WITHOUT END

W. Warren Wagar

'People well schooled in temporal studies, who routinely think in terms of processes of continuity and change occurring over la longue duree of earthly and cosmic time, instead of being glued all their lives on the the sticky flypaper of the present, will behave differently from inhabitants of the flypaper.'

The far future is not a fantasy. Nor is it without significance to the more than five billion of us now alive on earth. If our current understanding of the laws of physics and biology can be trusted at all, the far future will happen in one way and no other, and into that same uni-directional far future our sons and daughters and their sons and daughters will make their way, carrying traces of all of us, our atoms, our genes, our ideas, and our deeds, to the terminus of time.

To me this is a staggering thought. Not a complex or abstruse thought. It takes very little effort to generate. But I find it staggering, just the same, when I give it a chance to percolate through my consciousness. What could be more significant to us, here and now, than the realization that in this concrete, unquestionable, unmetaphysical sense, we are immortal – and therefore responsible – beings, worlds without end? The major positive religions have been constructed around mystical versions of this same vision. But no mysticism is involved here.

So the first, and perhaps most vital, reason for a far-future perspective is to connect us in imagination to our posterity, to Braudel's world of *la longue durée*. Braudel was concerned with matters like the age-old relationship of the peasant to the land, or the mariner to the sea, or the gradual evolution of capitalism over centuries of European life. The kings and the generals come and go, but what endures is the life of *la longue durée*, which, until recently, most historians tended to ignore, or consigned to a low place in the hierarchy of historical values. (Braudel, passim).

Plumbing the far future renders more vivid and urgent in our minds the sheer animal fact of our involvement in what will transpire long after we are dust.

Such awareness not only gives our lives more meaning, but also helps to make us more responsible human beings in the present. We may be less inclined, as a result, to run through reserves of irreplaceable minerals, less inclined to poison the biosphere, and more confidently resolved to invest in strategies and technologies that promise long-term rewards for all humankind, such as prolongevity research or the exploration of the solar system.

But developing far-future awareness is not easy. In our research, and above all in our schools and universities, we need to tap the resources of at least two more established disciplines: history and geology.

Futures inquiry of one kind or another has fascinated me since childhood. But since childhood I have also harboured a strong interest in these other two, which, together, profoundly enhance our sense of the reality of times other than our own fragile, fugitive present. We may even come to think of geology, history, and futures inquiry as all one discipline, which we could christen 'temporal studies', the exploration of the unfolding of time from the Archeozoic era, which began nearly four billion years ago, through the millennia of world history, to the millennia and the millions and billions of years of future time.

Past and future time have much in common. They are not present to our observation, they cannot be known in their fullness, they are inconceivably long, all of which separate them from us as we live and breathe in the present. Yet they are intensely real and consequential to every one of us. They are as real as the present – at one level, much more so. They define who we are and what we can hope to do.

Past and present are also of equal importance. We need to cultivate an understanding of both. Studying alternative futures without knowing all we can know of the past is no better than dwelling obsessively on past or present action without trying to imagine its consequences in future time. In this view, studies of past and future are mutually reinforcing; or rather they become so, as soon as we appreciate that there is no intrinsic difference between the two, except the position of the observer. Standing in the middle of a river and looking upstream, one sees the past. Standing in the middle of a river and gazing downstream, one sees the future. But it is always the same river.

People well schooled in temporal studies, who routinely think in terms of processes of continuity and change occurring over *la longue durée* of earthly and cosmic time, instead of being glued all their lives to the sticky flypaper of the present, will behave differently from inhabitants of the flypaper. In taking time seriously, they will also take their lives more seriously. Placing their lives in a temporal context, they will act more responsibly, more conservingly, more caringly, with more reverence not only for the past but for the future as well.

Clearly all this will not happen solely as the result of a proliferation of temporal studies in schools or anywhere else. Let us not overblow the importance of a sense of temporality in raising our collective consciousness. There are other ways of achieving similar results.

It is also true that 'temporalism', is carried beyond the bounds of common sense, can even be mortally dangerous. Those who take too rigid a view of time, imagining they know more than they do, can end by devaluing present life and happiness in the name of some imagined past or future felicity. Virtually all the totalitarian regimes of our century have been informed by a past-centered or future-centred ideology that tells their hapless subjects precisely what the past ordains or what the future demands. Such ideologies have driven living men and women to sacrifice themselves and other men and women (often quite uselessly) in the service of this or that time-centred and invariably wrong-headed dogma.

The only corrective to such idolatries of time is something that historians and geologists in our postmodern culture have come to realize and that most serious futurists have always assumed. That is, we do not literally *know* what happened in the past or what will happen in the future. We study alternative futures; but the same is true of historians and geologists, only they study alternative pasts.

The reason is not far to seek. The past, like the future, is not here, not accessible to us in present time. It cannot be reconstructed, event by event, in all its vastness and complexity and interconnectedness. Too little evidence survives and our capacities are too limited to enable us ever to build an exact replica in our minds and writings of any past era. Moreover we have learned from poststructuralist criticism that there is no single 'right' way to read a text, and no way at all to bridge the bridgeless chasm between symbols, such as words, and realities, such as the living, breathing Napoleon who fought for more than twenty years on the battlegrounds of Europe.

The best we can do is assemble what we believe into various plausible, alternative explanations, which will keep changing from year to year as fresh evidence becomes available, as old evidence disappears, and as our scholarly perspectives change and change again. This is what futurists do when they canvass the future – near-term, middle-term, or long-term, it matters little which. Futurists do not deal in knowledge, assuming such a thing is even possible in any field of inquiry. They deal in imaginables, or, better yet, in what the late Bertrand de Jouvenel called *futuribles*, future states that can be projected step by step from the most trustworthy data and the most cogent theories currently available to us. (de Jouvenel, 1967).

If we take into serious account our limitations as students of time, the consciousness we construct of the long-term past and future will not be anything rigid, dogmatic, or totalising. The details will vary from person to person, from culture to culture, from century to century. We will never be able to agree entirely on priorities or prospects; and various segments of the human race will take different paths, towards different goals.

But it is better to have some sense of direction, even if it keeps changing, than none. Better to design fallible and mutable agendas than none at all.

And what a lot of work we have to do. The long-term future, we may be sure, will not consist of endlessly multiplied doses of the present. Perhaps sooner than we think, the time will come when debates on abortion, wrangling about the status of the West Bank, oil wars in the Persian Gulf, clashes between Britain and Europe over the shape of the European Community, and all the rest, will no longer furrow human brows.

Such matters deserve our attention in the 1990s, of course. But if we stretch our minds to include the twenty-second century and the twenty-third, and the aeons of time remaining in this well-nigh infinite universe, other issues become far more important, issues that we can and should begin (and in some instances have begun) to address right now.

From our present perspective, these far-future concerns fall conveniently into two categories. One might be called the conquest of inner space, and the other the exploration and settlement of outer space. In the one case, our mission will be to understand and gain mastery of the 'microworld,' the world of the inconceivably small, the world of the DNA strand, the nucleus of the atom, and the engines no bigger than molecules that nanotechnologists (as Eric Drexler writes) may one day build in prodigious quantities to do most of humanity's work. In the other case, the exploration and settlement of outer space, our task will be in some ways much simpler. We have reliable maps of our likeliest destinations, and the technology to reach them is already *futurible*.

But we are far from marshalling the molecules of inner space. Apart from crude fission technologies, we have not yet learned how to release the stupendous energy locked in the atomic nucleus, such as the energy available in the isotopes of hydrogen or helium ('heavy' hydrogen and 'light' helium) that could give us unlimited cheap nuclear fusion power. Virologists have not yet succeeded in chaining or destroying the viruses that cause most of the worst diseases still afflicting our species. Gerontologists cannot give us life spans well past the century mark, although the secrets of ageing and rejuvenation lie under our noses in the cellular microworld, ready to be uncovered. Geneticists have only begun to map the human genome. Even when they are finished, they will still not know how each gene and genetic sub-unit operates to produce a complete human being with all of its unique flaws and miraculous powers. They are still further from being able to create life, or accelerate its evolution, or shape it to our heart's desires. Computer scientists working in the microworld of the silicon chip have yet to create machines capable of true intelligence, although some of them think they know how the trick will eventually be done, and how it will fundamentally transform our society.

Nevertheless! There can be no doubt, none at all, that in due course the explorers of the microworld will bring it under human control – for better or for worse, or both. Limitless energy, perfect health, long or even immortal life, new and higher (or lower) species of humanity, utopias of peace and happiness (or slavery and misery), and much more lie just beyond the horizons we can see today. Not only will they materialise, sooner or later, somewhere or somewhen, but they will have consequences of their own beyond our power to conceive.

The other frontier that must engage our best thoughts and efforts for millennia, and perhaps forever, is the frontier of outer space. Any intelligent person today understands that we live in a galaxy thickly populated with stars. Beyond our galaxy lie billions of other galaxies. To be sure, most scholars do nothing at all with this knowledge. Somehow, it fails to stir them. Mysteriously, they cannot see its relevance.

But consider. It is unthinkable that among these trillions of stars, sentient life evolved only on a single planet of our local star. Unthinkable that in all this immensity, there are no other planets suitable for human habitation. Unthinkable that in this rich and teeming cosmos, the resources do not exist for the building of numberless artificial worlds, orbiting or mobile, sun-tethered or free-roaming, in which the human race can continue its adventure wherever it pleases, until the end of time. The impact on our lives of encounters with extraterrestrial civilisations and the impact on our lives of the diffusion of humankind throughout the cosmos is beyond measuring. Such events will shrink all history hitherto almost to insignificance.

In short, we are no more than infants taking our first lungfuls of air. Most of history, the greatest part, much longer than the few thousand years of civilisation studied by historians, longer than the hundred thousand years of *Homo sapiens*, longer than even the 3.8 billion years since the dawn of the Archeozoic Era on Planet Earth – most of history is still waiting to happen.

But none of this devalues any of us, in present-day reality. Just the reverse. None of this devalues us because all of us now alive are the vital, indispensable links between what was and what will be. On our shoulders and ours alone, in this epoch, rests the heavy but also joyful burden of continuing the human adventure. To continue well, we must sharpen our vision, and gaze without fear or reserve into those far-distant files of time.

DIMENSIONS OF A NEW WORLD ORDER

Ervin Laszlo

'. . . we have the freedom to choose our destiny. The alternatives before us are evolution with distinction – or devolution, ultimately to extinction. The choice is real and it is ours.'

Today, unlike in the 1970s, attempting to create a world order is not a hopelessly utopian proposition. The end of the ideological divide between East and West removed a number of political obstacles to the formation and implementation of world-level goals and strategies; and the Gulf War has revealed the interdependence of contemporary nation-states and proved that even the most powerful among them cannot achieve major geopolitical, environmental, and financial objectives outside a multilateral context.

Rising concerns with the environment, with the activities of global corporations, with the stability of the world financial system, and with the promotion of worldwide economic development, joined with enduring concern for international peace and security, brought into fresh focus the concept of world order. It has been brought back on the international agenda by President George Bush, who was prompted to call for a new world order when, in the wake of the 1991 Gulf crisis, he was facing the task of creating order in the Middle East. Echoing his call have been not only international non-governmental organisations, many of which have long been intent on promoting steps that would lead to a new world order, but also forward-looking politicians both East and West.

The revival of the world order concept is also due to the realization that the alternative to some institutional form of order on the global level is either a one-sided dictatorship by the rich and powerful, or unbridled and unfair competition between the rich and the poor. While it is always possible that in the more distant future a spirit of solidarity would take hold of the thinking of leaders in government and business, thereby dispensing with the need for institutionalised forms of world order, in the near-term the danger of the unilateral domination by the privileged one-fourth of humanity of the under-privileged three-fourths cannot be ruled out.

THE FUNCTIONAL DOMAINS OF A NEW WORLD ORDER

A new world order presupposes agreement on the areas where it is to function. The principle by which to identify these areas has been enunciated by the Inter Action Council at its April 1990 meeting in Lisbon. The urgently needed new world order, said the former Heads of State and Government who make up the membership of the Council, must be characterised by the exercise of delegated sover-eignty based on the principle that decisions should be taken at the lowest possible level at which they can be effective.

There are many areas where the lowest possible level of decision-making is the local, and on these areas grass-roots governance is indicated. Other areas call for national or regional decision-making, and hence for action by national or regional governments. But there are also areas where the lowest possible level at which decisions could be effective is the global. These areas include international peace and security, the abolition of the colonisation of one state by another, the sheltering of international refugees, the combatting of the spread of drugs and terrorism, the provision of basic nutritional, educational and health resources and empoverished populations, minorities, refu-gees, and children, the management of the 'global commons' (the oceans, the atmosphere, Antarctica, and outer space), and the regula-tion of the world financial system.

When considering the overall dimensions of a new world order, three of these areas deserve close attention. These are: *the maintenance of international peace and security; the protection of the planetary environment;* and *the regulation of the world financial system.*

International peace and security   Peace and security are no longer the exclusive domain of nation-state policy decisions. National borders, especially of smaller countries, can often be more effectively safeguarded by a regional defence system than by a national army. This view is becoming increasingly operational in Europe. A Euro-pean Defence Community, rejected by France when it was first proposed in the 1960s, was revived in the 1980s in the framework of the CSCE (Conference on Security and Cooperation in Europe) and is now moving toward realisation as a European Defence Force. Germany and France champion the arrangement, and most other member states are in favour of it. Even Switzerland, where the army is a respected national institution, had second thoughts about maintaining a large and costly defence establishment, as shown by the surprising results of a 1990 popular referendum.

Since the demonstration of the effectiveness of collective peacekeeping in the Persian Gulf in 1991, even major powers have begun to look favourably on international peacekeeping arrangements. UN forces have repeatedly proved their effectiveness in hot-spots such as Cyprus, the Near and the Middle East, and in 1988 were honoured with the Nobel Peace Prize. Support for such forces is likely to grow in coming years, as economic problems force the reduction of national military budgets while security problems continue to plague the majority of national governments.

The protection of the environment   In the area of environmental protection, global-level action and decision-making have become well-nigh imperative. With regard to the global commons, such decision-making is already coming on line. The world's oceans and atmosphere, its outer space as well as its polar regions are obvious domains of global decision and action: on the one hand oceans, atmosphere, space and polar regions cannot be readily divided, appropriated, and nationally or privately owned, and on the other their integrity remains a precondition of ensuring humanly favourable conditions in the planetary environment. Conventions for the protection of extraterritorial waters, for safeguarding the chemical composition of gases in the atmosphere, for protecting and regulating the use of outer space, and for the integrity of the ecology of the Antarctic have already been signed, and many more are in preparation.

Global action with regard to the sovereign territories of individual states is more difficult. Significant development can be expected here on the one hand in the European Community, where the project of a European Environmental Agency is gathering momentum, and on the other at the 1992 UNCED (the United Nations Conference on Environment and Development), where the issue of a global ecological authority is likely to be on the agenda.

The world financial system   Of the three crucial domains where public policies need to become part of a new world order, that of world finance is the most recent. It is only in the past few years that national governments have become conscious that, just as they cannot protect their citizens from concerted external aggression by themselves and cannot shield their people from the effects of environmental degradation, they are also unable to protect their national economies from the harmful effects of unfavourable and unpredictable financial flows. The occasional summits of some heads of government and the ad hoc caucuses of a few heads of central banks are far from adequate to this task. Finance, like security and the environment, knows no national borders and does not respond to unilateral national measures – nor even to poorly orchestrated international initiatives.

It is becoming evident that, in order to stimulate economic growth, assure better equity among nations, and protect national economies from unpredictable and potentially disastrous stock-market and exchange rate fluctuations, better coordination is needed in public-sector interventions in world financial flows. As a result, the international financial system emerges as the third major functional domain of a new world order.

THE SPIRIT OF A REALISTIC WORLD ORDER

Governance at the global level, even if limited to specific functional domains, poses unparalleled problems and challenges to contemporary peoples and states. In the course of recorded history world-level leadership rested primarily on the exercise of military power. This was the case in the world empire of Alexander, and even in the relatively enduring Pax Romana created by the emperors of classical Rome. But today military power is not a basis for effective government: the failure of the Vietnam war and of the Iraqi annexation of Kuwait are eloquent testimony on this point, as are the collapse of the Soviet empire and Yugoslavia. In the late 20th century, world order can only rest on a deep-seated consensus regarding its legitimacy. Such consensus, in turn, calls for a high level of solidarity among the world's peoples.

How to bring about such solidarity in practice? The exercise of power, whether political or military, is useless, and so is mere exhortation and rhetoric. The required step seems to mobilize the principal forces that shape the minds of contemporary people.

The holistic alliance   After the French Revolution and the Napoleonic wars, European nations forged an alliance dedicated to the establishment of a community of the world's Christian nations. The 'Holy Alliance,' though it ultimately fell apart, stabilised Europe and created a system of collective security with lasting benefits.

The alliance required today, to forge a spirit of cooperation and solidarity among the world's peoples, must be both *holy* and *holistic*. It must be an alliance of science, the greatest source of creativity in contemporary culture, and of religion, the deepest source of human solidarity, with the people who make up the main body of world society.

Science has been shaping the modern mind in many known and countless unknown ways. That Western societies are left-brain dominated and its people think linearly in terms of causes and effects is due in no small measure to the influence of a form of rationality that, though now obsolete in the front lines of contemporary science, has seeped deeply into the public consciousness. Its consequences include a form of pragmatism that refuses to look beyond what can be seen and touched, and bought and consumed. This tends to make people unaware of the more distant and long-term consequences of their actions, and therefore unconcerned and irresponsible about them.

Many contemporary scientists persist, however, in viewing the interaction between science and society as an unwelcome fetter. Science, in their view, is a search for truth, or at least for a better understanding of observable reality, and it must be free of demands and constraints of any kind. These scientists are intent to keep away from what Galileo in his time called 'the passions that divide men.'

The ideal of an aloof and disinterested science has historical roots, going back to the origins of modern scientific thinking in the 16th and 17th centuries. At that time the humanistic culture of Europe had difficulty extricating itself from the domination of the medieval Church and scientists could engage in their enquiries and experiments only if they did not intrude on the sacred authority of the Pope. The trials of Giordano Bruno and of Galileo were ample proof of the wish of the Church of Rome to suppress, or at least to channel, scientific enquiry. The new empirical sciences could exist and evolve only by professing independence from, and disinterest in, the affairs of society.

But in the late 20th century there is no need for scientists to seek refuge in isolation and neutrality; no high authority questions the legitimacy of the scientific enterprise. Science could recognize its ties with society and become humanly committed; this would not call for relinquishing the ideal of scientific freedom. Such freedom is relative in any case: as long as scientists remain dependent on society for pursuing their investigations (and already for obtaining their training), progress in science will be influenced by social priorities. And as long as scientists produce ideas and theories that have implications or applications for the life of individuals and the prosperity of societies, the enterprise of science will remain an agent of social change.

Recognising the ties that exist between science and society would be desirable for science and essential for society. On the one hand it would make for less bias in science's enquiry into the nature of the observable world; and on the other it would make for a more responsible application of the results of scientific enquiry in society. And, above all, given the objective need for globally coordinated action in a number of policy domains, a new alliance between science and society would furnish solid reasons and enduring legitimacy for global cooperation, and for the solidarity that is its precondition.

The alliance between religion and society would be just as important as the alliance regarding science. There is more to human beings than scientific reason can satisfy: there is also an intuition of higher meaning and transcendental significance, and a sense of the sacred that recurs in all cultures and societies. Religious belief systems respond to these insights and intuitions. People may not adhere to any doctrine or visit any church, mosque, synagogue or temple, yet be influenced by Christian, Moslem, Judaic, Hindu, Buddhist, Taoist, Confucian or other religious values and worldviews. Religion, as even the American pragmatist philosopher William James was led to conclude, gives scope to the universal human capacity to go beyond the world of the senses and enter into union with a higher reality. (James 1974, 1976)

The insight and intuition of the world religions would be crucial in inspiring people with the kind of solidarity that is essential for the creation of an enduring world order. Religious communities, living up to the original meaning of their name *religare* (binding together) could inspire a universal ethic of sharing and solidarity among their followers.

There is a humanistic and ecumenical strand in all the world religions, even if the practice of some religious communities ignores or subverts it. At the heart of Christian teaching, for example, is love for a universal God that must be reflected in love for one's fellows and service to one's neighbour. Islam has a universal and ecumenical aspect as well: *tawhid*, the affirmation of unity, means the religious witness 'there is no god but Allah' where Allah is the symbol of divine presence and revelation for all people. Judaism sees man as God's partner in the ongoing work of creation and calls on the people of Israel to be 'a light to the nations,' while Hinduism perceives the essential oneness of mankind within the oneness of the universe. Buddhism has as its central tenet the interrelatedness of all things in 'dependent co-origination,' interpreted by progressive Buddhists as a mandate for achieving higher forms of unity in a world of interdependence, and the Chinese spiritual traditions revere harmony as a supreme principle of nature and society. In Confucianism harmony applies to human relationships in ethical terms, while in Taoism harmony is an almost aesthetic concept defining nature, and the relationship between man and nature. And the Baha'i faith sees the whole of mankind as an organic element in the process of inevitable evolution toward unity and peace.

Bringing to the fore the humanistic and ecumenical element of religious traditions would not impair the orthodoxy of their doctrines; it would only make the doctrines more relevant. After all, the great prophets were spiritually and socially relevant to *their* times. It is now up to their followers to make sure that their teachings remain relevant to ours.

The culture of interexistence   Global solidarity need not lead to global uniformity. That science gives rational grounds and legitimacy to world-level cooperation, and that religion provides the emotional underpinning and spiritual insight for it, does not mean that the diversity of the world's peoples and cultures would be destroyed. People and cultures can remain different from one another and yet have real understanding for, and deep solidarity with, one another. Diversity in the human world is just as necessary as diversity in nature – in both spheres uniformity would reduce resilience and become the prelude to decline and extinction.

However, more is needed in the 21st century than a mere tolerance of diversity. Letting people *be* what they want 'as long as they stay in their part of the world,' and letting them *do* what they want 'as long as they don't do it in my backyard' are obsolete attitudes. In the contemporary world different people and different societies must learn to live together, completing and complementing one another. People and societies must do better than co-exist – they must 'interexist.'

Interexistence denotes an active, mutually constitutive relationship, instead of a passive, purely external one. It suggests that it is possible for individuals, societies, enterprises, and entire cultures to exist not merely side by side, but *with* and *through* each other. The concept is relevant not only to East-West relations, but to the enterprise of a new world order as a whole.

Interexistence is inclusive: its logic is you *and* I, they *and* we. It replaces the logic of egotism and exclusion which says me *or* you; we *or* they. The new logic can enable people and societies to play 'positive sum' win-win games. As long as the players see each other's interests

as merely offsetting each other, they will engage in zero-sum games –
the win of one will be the loss of the other, so that the sum of the wins
and losses equals zero. But when the players perceive that their
existence is interdependent and their interests coincide, they will find
games where the win of one is also the win of the other. There are
many such games: the principal ones are peace, economic development, and a healthy environment. The way to play these games is to
do away with nuclear, biological, chemical, and the more deadly
varieties of conventional weapons and create a joint peacekeeping
system; to have fewer children in rapidly growing high-fertility
populations; to share useful skills, technologies, and capital with
poorer or less developed partners; to channel investment to education, communication, and human resource development as well as to
the building of basic economic and social infrastructures; and to
respect the balances and thresholds that are vital to the integrity of
nature and the future of humanity.

Creating a new world order is an unprecedented challenge. It needs
to be met, however, if human survival and development on this
planet are to be assured. The challenge embraces the identification of
the areas where global decision-making and action are necessary, and
of the actions to which priority will have to be given when it comes to
implementation. The cultural and spiritual dimensions of the new
order must not be neglected either: without significant growth in the
reciprocal solidarity of contemporary peoples and governments the
best thought-out plans will remain but paper tigers.

Given a significant growth in human solidarity, and international
agreement on the domains where world-level action is the *sine qua non*
of development and progress, concrete attention could focus on
building up the institutional mechanisms through which such action
can be designed and implemented.

The prospect of a string of international organisations regulating
more and more aspects of human activity fills many people with
misgivings. The public fears the spectre of distant and unfeeling
bureaucracies issuing edicts and impacting on their lives and free-
doms, and governments are unwilling to yield up any part of the
sovereignty which they consider their inalienable right. However,
such fears and reluctance are not justified if the new institutional
mechanisms confine themselves to the specific domains where action
is irremediably ineffective below the global level. A world security
system, an ecological authority, and a financial coordinatory and
regulatory body would serve every nation's interest – and would
allow full scope for the autonomy of national and local decision-
making in all other policy domains.

Setting up the required institutional mechanisms is a challenge first of all to the United Nations, humanity's only duly constituted universal organization. The UN system would have to undertake integrated action in the key world order domains notwithstanding the current fragmentation of its authority among relatively autonomous organs and agencies.

The transformation of the United Nations from a loosely-knit system of semi-independent and frequently competing sub-units to an organic whole serving the world community is new to the agenda of its reform. Since the end of the 1960s the world body has been the subject of numerous studies and discussions, both by individual scholars and formally mandated commissions. But the majority of the recommendations, including those framed by the Jackson and the Pierson Reports, focused on the efficiency of the UN and on procedural and organisational issues; they assumed the basic tasks to have been adequately described in the UN Charter. However, as the Director-General of UNESCO said at a high-level cabinet meeting in April, 1991: 'It is no longer enough to confine our efforts to trying to make the system more effective; it is also necessary to make it more relevant.'

AN INFERNAL STRATEGY REVIEW

James Robertson

The attached document came to me recently without explanation, from a source which I have been unable to trace. It carries no date, but internal evidence suggests it was written in 1991. It embodies a vision for the 21st century – and beyond. The future to which it is committed is not the future to which most of us look forward. On its own terms it is optimistic, but most of us may well draw pessimistic conclusions from its optimism.

It suggests also that thinking about the future has to be geared towards action. Each one of us is positively responsible for helping to create the future, within the constraints of our own circumstances and capacities. We help to create it, both by our actions and by our inactions. This is a freedom and a responsibility that humans cannot escape.

James Robertson, i.iv.1992

MEMORANDUM TO THE PRESIDENT

RE: STRATEGY FOR THE NEXT CENTURY AND THE NEXT MILLENNIUM

After the last Stygian Council meeting a hundred years ago, You asked us to review infernal strategy for the next century and the next millennium. This is a summary of our report. It is for discussion at the forthcoming Council meeting.

Since the Council first met several millennia ago we have steadfastly pursued the goal we then agreed. This was well summarised by a Mr. Milton in a report on those early events. That report, titled *Paradise Lost*, is quite recent and You may not yet have had time to read it. Milton describes our aim as 'seducing the race of Man' into 'wasting God's whole creation' to the point where He 'with repenting hand would abolish His own works' – an accurate reflection of our self-appointed task.

We are able to report good progress over the past few hundred years. The cancerous impact of the human species on itself and on the ecosystems of the Earth has now well and truly taken hold – to the point where it could soon prove terminal. This offers us the prospect of an important victory over the Enemy. We can take satisfaction from it.

However, we must not be complacent. As increasing numbers of humans come to recognise the gravity of the world crisis they are creating (with our concealed assistance), they might be inspired to halt their stampede toward the abyss. They could still change direction just in time to thwart our Plan.

The following is a possible scenario. A United Nations Conference on Environment and Development is to be held in June 1992 in Brazil. This Earth Summit will be a historic event. For the first time ever the peoples of the world will meet together to discuss their 'common future'. And 1992 will be a historic year. It will be the 500th anniversary of Columbus' voyage to the western hemisphere. That voyage marked the beginning of the modern Euro-American period of human history, which now promises to culminate in the global disaster for which we have been working. The suggestion is that, when such a historic meeting in such a historic year confronts humans with the occasion for worldwide reflection and repentance, this will bring them to their senses; and that then the approach of 'The Year

2000', which many of them will see as the time for a millennial breakthrough, will strengthen their determination to switch to a different path of progress for the future.

We have examined this scenario and understand it, but we do not find it realistic. The pressures of career competition and survival in business and finance and politics and government around the world will almost certainly be strong enough to frustrate the success (from the human point of view) of the Earth Summit. Furthermore, in this as in other matters of concern to us, our infernal skills of disinformation and public relations will keep the professional communicators on our side. We can rely on the world's media to ignore the potential significance of the Earth Summit until it is actually taking place, and then to concentrate on its entertainment value rather than the serious issues at stake.

Nonetheless, we recommend that infernal observers watch very carefully the efforts humans make in the next few years to change their present path of development. We should continue to encourage them to play down the severity of the risks they now face. We should persuade them that prudence and good judgment call for delay until scientists and economists can agree on what needs to be done. (We can rely on economists to argue for many years about what 'sustainable development' actually means.) For the longer term we must make sure that the efforts which humans eventually make to achieve sustainability are positively counter-productive.

In that respect we must follow the pattern of our previous successes. We contrived to persuade humans to transform the Christian atonement of 2000 years ago into the service of their own material ambitions and struggles for power. We helped them to transform the initial journeys of Christian explorers from Europe 500 years ago into a worldwide wave of destruction, in which many peoples and cultures and biological species have perished – and continue to perish today. In the last two or three hundred years we have successfully encouraged them to transform the scientific revolution and the 'Enlightenment', on which they originally embarked with such high moral and spiritual purpose, into more powerful engines of physical and moral and spiritual destruction and waste than have ever existed before. We have helped them to redefine 'the creation of wealth' as a competitive struggle for supremacy and survival among themselves, and to redefine 'economy' as a compulsive addiction to unnecessary extraction and wastage of nature's resources.

These are no mean achievements. The challenge is to live up to them now. But this should not be beyond our powers.

Influential human leaders are already calling for 'a new wave of

175363

economic growth' to deal with the problems that past economic growth has caused. What might have been dangerous ideas like democracy and development have already been converted into instruments – like the 'free market' and 'free trade' – through which rich and powerful people can dominate and disable the poor and weak. In the last few years, concern with sustainable development has itself mushroomed into an unsustainably wasteful bonanza of parasitical busyness – national and international conferences, consultations, publications, research, and so on. Mad scientists, dreaming of nuclear reactors in 50 years' time which will generate heat 2000 times hotter than the sun, are given serious attention; while sober engineers, capable of providing all the energy humans need by a mixture of energy efficiency, energy conservation and renewable energy supply, are dismissed as unreliable cranks. (Our experts from the Ministry of Destruction and Science and the Ministry of Disinformation and Public Relations are asking for increased budgets to step up their successful cooperation in this area.) Meanwhile leading humans, by simultaneously paying themselves huge salaries and preaching the virtues of wage restraint, elegantly combine encouragement of financial greed with the promotion of widespread cynicism. (You recently recognised the brilliance of our infernal task force in this area by bestowing a Satan's Award for Excellence on the relevant division in the Ministry of Waste and Economic Affairs.)

In these and many other ways things are going well. With discreet help from us, the human race seems hell-bent on its own destruction and the destruction, if not of a very large part of the Universe, of enough of the Enemy's creation to be well worth our while.

As You know, the question has been raised whether this would necessarily turn out to be a victory for us. Might not the self-destruction of the human species and its environment, like the past destruction of earlier species (e.g. the dinosaurs), create conditions in which new, more advanced forms of life and consciousness would eventually emerge on Earth? Might we not then feel that – far from our having triumphed over the Enemy – He had skilfully out-manoeuvred us?

We reject that doubt for two reasons. First, more advanced forms of life and consciousness would, in fact, widen the future scope for infernal subversion of the Enemy's creation – *corruptio optimi pessima*, as His supporters say. That is an outcome we would welcome. Second, the disaster threatening the human species is now so imminent that their successful avoidance of it might well be interpreted as a defeat for us. That is an outcome we would want to avoid.

To conclude then, our unanimous recommendation is that infernal

0490972

strategy should encourage humans to continue on their present catastrophic course. We seek the Council's agreement and Your authority to proceed accordingly.

B.L.Z. Bubb   (Minister, Planning)
M. Ammon   (Minister, Waste and Economic Affairs)
M.O. Loch   (Minister, Destruction and Science)
B.E. Lial   (Minister, Disinformation and Public Relations).

AN IMPOSSIBLE DREAM?

Robert Muller

I dream
That on 1 January 2000
The whole world will stand still
In prayer, awe and gratitude
For our beautiful, heavenly Earth
And for the miracle of human life.

I dream
That young and old, rich and poor,
Black and white,
Peoples from North and South,
From East and West.
From all beliefs and cultures
Will join their hands, minds and hearts
In an unprecedented, universal
Bimillennium Celebration of Life.

I dream
That the year 2000
Will be declared World Year of Thanksgiving
by the United Nations.

I dream
That during the year 2000
Innumerable celebrations and events
Will take place all over the globe
To gauge the long road covered by humanity
To study our mistakes
And to plan the feats
Still to be accomplished
For the full flowering of the human race
In peace, justice and happiness.

I dream
That the few remaining years
To the Bimillennium
Be devoted by all humans, nations and institutions
To unparalleled thinking, action,
Inspiration, elevation,
Determination and love
To solve our remaining problems
And to achieve
A peaceful, united human family on Earth.

WAR IS A DYING BUSINESS

Keith Suter

*'The strongest nation in the world is the nation which can convert its enemy
into its friend – and, better still, its trading partner.'*

A WORLD WITHOUT WAR

> War was the glory of my childhood. I must confess there was not a hint of
> moral outrage in my being, nor have I ever been a pacifist. I could say with
> Franklin Roosevelt: 'I hate war'; I can say that I have feared war; but until
> nuclear war was born, I never believed in a world without war. Now no
> other kind of world is imaginable. (Salisbury, 1983)

This change within the veteran *New York Times* journalist provides
the theme for this chapter. There is a gradual decline in the reliance on
war as an instrument of national policy. The decline is not a deliberate
move by governments to work for general and complete disarmament. It is, rather, a reducing utility in war itself as a way of solving
political disputes. Similarly, there is only a gradual move towards
greater use of alternative methods for settling disputes.

The declining reliance on war has been underway for some
decades. It has been obscured by other events. The mass media
concentrate on drama and colour, and slogans and phrases (such as
'glasnost' and 'perestroika'). But behind all this gloss and glitter are
incremental changes which will eventually constitute a new edifice: a
new world order based on conflict resolution. It may be difficult to
envisage such a different world – but it is no more difficult than to
imagine a planet after World War III.

It is necessary, then, to make this unpublicized evolution explicit. Governments need to be encouraged to recognize that war is of declining usefulness and that it is in their interest to pay greater attention to conflict resolution.

I wish to make four points. First, conventional warfare is of declining usefulness. Second, nuclear weapons are also of little use for settling disputes. But as a contrast to all this good news, there is the third point: a warning about the growth of guerrilla warfare. Finally, you cannot do today's job with yesterday's methods and still be in business tomorrow. Consequently, this chapter ends with three sets of complementary ideas on alternative ways of settling disputes.

CONVENTIONAL WARFARE

Conventional warfare used to be about soldiers killing soldiers. In recent decades it has changed to machines killing machines. Soldiers are cheap: parents supply fresh personnel regularly. But machines are expensive. Nations can no longer afford to fight protracted conventional wars.

Warfare used to be a small and intimate affair. Guerrilla groups raided villages or fought each other. There was no need to wear uniforms because the fighters knew their comrades – anyone they did not recognize they could kill. Guerrilla warfare was the most common form of warfare around the globe.

About four centuries ago, warfare started to become larger. Europe, which pioneered conventional warfare, rediscovered the Roman tradition of organized fighting formations, uniforms and the system of ranks. But, operating with populations, industrial bases and revenues far larger than were ever available to Rome, Europe elevated conventional warfare to a new level of human enterprise. It set a pattern which has been copied around the world.

During the last four centuries the overall intention remained constant: soldiers killed soldiers. Wars were fought mainly away from civilian areas (except for sieges of towns). There was a cycle of combat determined by the weather. Land battles were fought between late spring and early autumn, when the ground was hard and the weather warm. Very few major operations were conducted in the winter; this was the time for sieges when mobility was unimportant.

World Wars I and II were the culmination of this tradition. Some features changed during the Wars. More importantly, even though conventional warfare has remained in existence since 1945, its utility has been declining.

Although World War II ended in 1945 peace did not break out for the military-industrial complexes in the new super powers. The US has a military-industrial complex – the USSR was a military-industrial complex. The Cold War (1945-90) resulted in no World War III as such – but the arms race helped destroy the USSR and gravely weakened the US. Japan won the Cold War. It has no military-industrial complex.

World War I's carnage encouraged the development of novel techniques to crash through the enemy's trenches, such as the tank. This process was accelerated in World War II. Conventional warfare therefore became a matter of machines killing machines.

One disadvantage of this reliance upon sophisticated weaponry is its cost. The defence industry has itself assumed a major role in defining weapons procurement policies and national security. A group of corporation and government decision-makers with narrow views and shared expectations has created new generations of increasingly expensive weapons systems of dubious effectiveness – with the inevitable rise in defence budgets. There is an iron triangle: the interlocking boards of directors, many with direct government experience; the interlocking interests of defence firms, financial institutions and auditors; and the revolving door of personnel between the Pentagon and industry. (Adams, 1982)

A second disadvantage is the way in which forces become mesmerized by their own weaponry. They lack the doubts about it that newcomers to such technology have. 'Testing' of such weaponry is done via static ground tests or by running key data through a computer which may or may not reveal flaws. Since each new missile system could cost around $50 million (minus warhead), it is too expensive to test the real thing.

This mesmerization becomes hubris. The USSR invaded Afghanistan in 1979 confident that its modern equipment would defeat the guerrillas. It was wrong. For example, guerrillas could hear the tanks lumbering up the mountain passes and so they rolled rocks to stop the tanks. As they stopped, the guerrillas shoved rags up their exhaust pipes and stalled the engines. They trapped the tanks and disposed of them as they wanted (such as setting alight to them and their crews).

Conventional equipment is also vulnerable to disruption. In April 1980, the US tried to release its 53 hostages held in Tehran. The helicopters flew into Iran without detection – but three of them (out of eight) developed mechanical problems. The raid was aborted with the loss of eight personnel.

These factors mean that conventional wars have to be brief. A conventional war has to be won in six weeks – or it may become a stalemate. The Iran-Iraq war, which began in 1979, dragged on for almost a decade and resulted in about a million deaths. Neither side could muster enough force to knock the other out of the war.

On the other hand, the 1991 Gulf War was over in 43 days. But what did the war settle? President Hussein was forced to realize that he could not use the military to take over Kuwait. President Bush won the war but lost the peace. When the Kurds rebelled (believing he would help them), they received no help: the US did not want to destroy the nation of Iraq because Iran or Syria (neither of which is pro-US) would fill the vacuum. The US did not want to remove President Hussein because it had no pro-US replacement for him.

The good news in all this tragedy is how rare such conventional wars are: 1979 onset of the Iran-Iraq war and the Soviet invasion of Afghanistan, 1982 the Falklands war, and 1991 the Gulf War.

NUCLEAR WEAPONS

The 1945 atomic bombs represented another major change in war-fare. One bomb could do the work of an entire air force operation. The neat distinction, according to the Red Cross Geneva Conventions, between legitimate targets (such as tanks, aircraft and ships) and protected personnel (such as prisoners of war) suddenly disappeared. An atomic attack would be so destructive that that sort of distinction was impossible.

The intention with nuclear weapons however, is not to win a war – but to deter one. Nuclear deterrence that works 99.999 per cent of the time is a failure. One problem with nuclear deterrence is the risk of political miscalculation – as occurred in 1914 when Germany did not expect the UK to enter the war.

A second problem is that humans have become hostages to technological reliability. Computers can fail because of design faults, a lack of adequate maintenance, and humans operating under the influence of alcohol or narcotics. The US and Soviet record for reliability elsewhere is not inspiring, such as Three Mile Island, Chernobyl and fatal space missions.

A third problem is derived from the peculiar concept of deterrence itself: what is being 'deterred' by nuclear deterrents? One nation's 'deterrent' is another nation's source of fear. The best way for the latter to reduce its fear is to increase its own deterrence – and this adds to a sense of fear in the other nation. The nuclear arms race is a race without end – or until something fails.

As the two superpowers (and to a lesser extent, the UK, France and China) siphoned off scientists to work on the arms race, so the arms race became a marginal – if very expensive – undertaking. The two superpowers could destroy the world several times over – but, in the meantime, the world's population bought Japanese cars and cameras.

Even though videotaping was invented in the US, the lengthy and expensive research and development process for the consumer-oriented video cassette recorder was done in Japan. Even the VCRs that carry American household brand names like RCA and Sears are made in Japan.

Even western financial institutions ignored the arms race. Western banks lent money to eastern Europe, US mid-west farmers sold grain to the USSR, and West Germany undertook to build a gas pipeline from Siberia to western Europe. Western transnational corporations invested in eastern Europe, where there were low labour costs and no 'communists' in the unions to organize strikes.

In the end, the only thing being protected by the arms race was the arms race itself. It institutionalized the injustices in eastern Europe the US was pledged to remove. Nuclear deterrence valued stability over justice. US nuclear weapons could not help Poland's Solidarity movement or the domestic critics inside the USSR.

The change began in March 1985, when Mr Gorbachev became the Soviet leader. He could see the damage the arms race was doing to the USSR and so he unilaterally began to reduce the Soviet military-industrial complex, by for example withdrawing from Afghanistan. What began as a communist reform resulted six years later in the end of communist rule.

But at least Mr Gorbachev was one step ahead of President Reagan. He knew that every weapon built in the USSR 'exploded' in the USSR – in the shabby buildings, inadequate nutrition and lack of consumer goods.

President Reagan and now President Bush have yet to make a similar acknowledgement about the US economy and the diversion of scientific personnel. According to Professor Seymour Melman of New York, it would cost over $7 trillion to refurbish the US economic infrastructure (from roads and bridges to factories) to become truly competitive with Japan and Germany – this is roughly the cost of the total US military expenditure for the entire Cold War. (Geneva, 1991)

With the USSR defeated, the US can now afford to learn the lesson of Japan and start rebuilding its economy. The world may now be heading into an era of reduced military expenditure.

A WARNING ABOUT GUERRILLA WARFARE

My chapter has dealt so far with two positive developments. It is necessary, however, not to become too optimistic. Although the world is now likely to avoid the World War III which was being speculated about a decade ago, guerrilla warfare is making a return.

The extent to which guerrilla warfare overshadows the world will be determined partly by the world's ability to develop conflict resolution techniques.

Guerrilla warfare is the world's oldest form of warfare but was only marginal in World Wars I and II. Lawrence of Arabia proved to his sceptical British Army colleagues that it could be used by the Arabs against the Turks. But his well publicized campaign was only a sideshow of a sideshow. Similarly, the European resistance to Hitler represented only a small percentage of the overall warfare.

Guerrilla warfare has become a growth industry since 1945. Every conflict underway today is of a guerrilla nature. There are urban guerrilla campaigns, such as the IRA in Northern Ireland, the ETA Basque separatists in Spain, and the Sendero Luminoso (Shining Path) in Peru. Rural examples include the Tamil Tigers of Sri Lanka fighting for an independent Eelam, the Sikhs in India fighting for a separate Khalistan, and the JKLF rebelling in Kashmir against Indian rule.

Guerrilla warfare challenges the prevailing paradigm of conventional warfare. Immense fire-power, large military expenditure and sophisticated weapons are not guarantees of victory – as the US found in Vietnam and the USSR in Afghanistan. A well organized and well motivated group fighting on its own terrain with the support of the local population is almost impossible to defeat.

Guerrilla warfare is the war of the flea. An elephant's foot can crush a flea – but more often the flea will hover around and irritate the elephant. Guerrilla groups can have an impact disproportionate to their size. Abu Nidal's Palestinian group has at no point ever had more than 500 fighters but it has conducted a programme of both selective assassination of key Israeli and other personnel and mass randomized attacks, such as the death of 13 people at Rome Airport in December 1985 and the September 1986 attack on an Istanbul synagogue which resulted in 22 deaths. He was also a prime suspect for the PanAm bomb blast in December 1988 over Lockerbie which resulted in 270 deaths. He has operated since 1974 and has evaded capture. He has not forced the Israelis to hand control of their land over to his fellow Palestinians – but he has irritated Israel.

Guerrilla warfare has increased for six reasons. First, it is the warfare of the weak against the strong. The defeat of European colonial powers in Asia by Japan in the early 1940s – even though it was only a temporary defeat – showed colonial peoples that Europeans were not necessarily destined to rule in Africa and Asia. They rebelled against their colonial masters and in every case eventually won – sometimes by using guerrilla warfare.

Second, modern weapons are often suited to unskilled groups. Hand-held missiles, for example, enable a soldier to attack an aircraft. More basically, Afghan guerrillas blunted Soviet tank operations with rocks and rags.

Third, as modern life has become more sophisticated so it has become more vulnerable to disruption. Two centuries ago, for example, each house in England had to look after its own water supply – and so each household was far more self-sufficient than today's reliance on a centralized reticulation system. A guerrilla group could not disrupt a town's water supply two centuries ago – nowadays it could.

Fourth, modern transport is of great use to guerrillas. It gives them greater mobility. It also provides targets (particularly airport lounges) since security is difficult to maintain in large buildings with a transitory population.

Fifth, the mass media publicise guerrilla attacks. Although comparatively few people are killed in these attacks, the deaths attract a disproportionate amount of news coverage. More Americans are killed on roads each year than the total number of Americans killed in Vietnam – but this would not be inferred from the extensive coverage of that war. In almost every year since 1969 more people have been killed on Northern Ireland roads than killed that year in the guerrilla warfare – but, again, the war gets the greater coverage. The world is watching. Television companies are getting the drama of a Hollywood production without having to pay Hollywood rates.

Finally, since imitation is the sincerest form of flattery, there is the risk that governments could use guerrilla warfare for attacks on other nations. Conventional warfare is too expensive and nuclear warfare too suicidal. Guerrilla warfare could be a cheap way of disrupting a political opponent.

The extent to which the globe can capitalize upon the declining utility of coventional and nuclear warfare and simultaneously avoid a further growth of guerrilla warfare depends partly on the growth of conflict resolution as a way of settling disputes.

GREATER SECURITY WITH FEWER WEAPONS

There is now a peace race. On the one hand, there is less reliance upon conventional warfare and nuclear weapons. On the other hand, there is a growing risk of ethnic disputes, border clashes and guerrilla warfare. Can we build upon the former and prevent the latter from escalating?

This will require a fresh way of thinking about warfare. Too often in the past the world has followed the principle: if you want peace, prepare for war. The futility of this approach is reflected in a statement by John Adams, US President in 1790:

> I must study politics and war, that my . . . (children) . . . may study mathematics and philosophy, geography, natural history and naval architecture, navigation, commerce and agriculture, in order to give their children a right to study painting, poetry, music, architecture, statuary, tapestry and porcelain. (Barash & Lipton, 1982)

The real lesson is: if you prepare for war, you will get war.

We need to get away from missile envy: our infatuation with military technology. Even if nuclear weapons had not been invented, the world would still be in danger because other weapon systems would have been developed, such as larger chemical weapons or even more destructive conventional weapons. The real cause of war is not the availability of weapons but the underlying political tensions and our inability to find alternative ways of settling disputes.

The strongest nation in the world is the nation which can convert its enemy into its friend – and, better still, its trading partner.

This chapter ends with three sets of ideas of complementary ways of enhancing security with fewer weapons: the peaceful settlement of international disputes, building peaceful relations, and creating ministeries for peace.

PEACEFUL SETTLEMENT OF INTERNATIONAL DISPUTES

In 1945, the United Nations outlawed war. All nations joining the UN agreed not to use force (or the threat of force) in settling disputes. As shown by the continued number of conflicts, governments have ignored that pledge.

It is necessary to give peace a chance. There is a wide range of options. The tragedy, then, is not that there are no alternatives to war (there are) – but that they are not used.

A dispute may be settled by the use of 'good offices'. For example, following the failure of the US rescue mission in Iran, Algeria volunteered to act as a go-between: it is a Moslem country and so is trusted by Iran; and it sells its oil to the west and so is trusted by the US. It secured the release of the hostages in January 1981. Similarly, the UN Secretary-General was invited by Mr Gorbachev to negotiate the USSR's withdrawal from Afghanistan.

If a dispute is essentially legal, then it could be referred to the International Court of Justice. The ICJ has, for example, made decisions on border disputes between nations.

All this work aims at both the immediate avoidance of war and the resolution of the long-term issues which have brought the nations into disagreement. It does not seek, therefore, merely to reaffirm the existing situation; it does not seek peace at any price. After all, merely to seek peace by papering over substantial differences invites the recurrence of the dispute. It seeks, instead, to resolve deep-seated issues to remove as far as possible the threat to security.

BUILDING PEACEFUL RELATIONSHIPS

It is necessary for nations to emphasize points of similarity rather than differences. Within nations this same approach should be used as a form of bringing people together – rather than acting in such a way as to permit the nation to fall apart in ethnic and other divisions.

A 1958 film *The Defiant Ones*, provides an example of this point. Two prisoners, one black (Sidney Poitier) and one white (Tony Curtis) have escaped from a prison in the southern US and are chained together. Each hates the other. But since they are chained together at the wrist, each can only outrun the hounds and posse providing the other is equally fleet of foot. The death or injury of one would mean the capture of the other.

> Chained together, they are compelled to cross a swift and dangerous river. At one point, the lead person loses his footing and both are swept away into the rapids. Finally, Tony Curtis manages to grab a branch and pull them towards the shore. Lying exhausted on the beach, Sidney Poitier gasps. 'Thanks for pulling me out'.
>
> Tony Curtis barks back. 'Man, I didn't pull you out; I kept you from pulling me in'. (Barash & Lipton 1982)

This approach can be illustrated by reference back to the Cold War. This was the central defining event of the period from 1945 to 1990. It was also a period of missed opportunities and of diversions provoked by the military-industrial complex in each nation. By contrast, if the Martians had invaded Earth in (say) 1981, the US and USSR would have lost no time in forming an alliance to meet the common threat – the proof of this assertion is the way in which they came together in 1941 to fight Nazi Germany.

The US should have adopted a 'greater goal' tactic during the Cold War in which the US invited the USSR to co-operate in working together in tasks with potential benefits much greater than the continued arms race, let alone the outcome of a World War III.

The example of food showed the paradoxes in the US-USSR

relationship. Although it was the world's largest wheat producer, the USSR did not produce enough to satisfy domestic demand. The USSR had to import wheat. Kansas farmers were politically conservative but their surplus-producing efficiency kept alive the USSR's communism. Indeed in the nuclear era, where no nation can directly defend itself from a nuclear attack, the Kansas farmers provided the US with some form of 'defensive cover', since it would have been suicidal for the USSR to destroy its primary source of imported wheat!

But instead of building upon this relationship, the US continued to see the USSR in a poor light – and so it brought out the worst in the USSR's paranoia. The US, on the contrary, should have found ways of bringing out better Soviet intentions. This it could have done by offering to help Soviet agriculture.

Continuing this hypothetical example, if the US had reduced some of its excessive military expenditure, then the funds thus saved could have been used to purchase durable consumer goods (manufactured in the Third World – to help their financial problems and to repay their debts to western banks) and offered as outright gifts to the Soviet people, for example, colour television sets. The USSR and the rest of eastern Europe represent a new frontier for consumer goods. This proposed policy would have had three benefits for ending the Cold War. First, words are cheap – people would have taken more notice of stated sincerity if supported by gifts. Second, the Soviet government would have had to admit that it and the US were working for a greater goal: a better material standard of living for the Soviet people. Third, it would have helped lock the USSR into the world's international economic system.

Ironically, the Cold War did end – and neither side was prepared for it. Instead of a planned conversion of military facilities to civilian use, there has only been a series of ad hoc decisions. We have ended the Cold War – but not gained a satisfactory peace.

We need to learn the lesson of the Cold War – and set out deliberately to build peaceful relationships rather than adversarial ones.

MINISTRY FOR PEACE

To handle this new era, we need to institutionalise the peace perspective in government. There is, for example, a distinct treasury perspective in all government deliberations involving financial considerations (usually to the extent of opposing as much proposed expenditure as possible). There is a distinct social welfare perspective (usually in favour of extending the government's mantle of care over its citizens). There is not, however, a distinct peace perspective. There is no cabinet minister specifically engaged on peacecraft activities.

In particular, the new Ministry would have three main areas of work: redefining 'national security', disarmament, and peacebuilding.

'National security' is more than just armed forces – the prime concern of the department of defence. It is more than just diplomacy and the maintenance of healthy international political arrangements – the prime concern of ministries of foreign affairs.

We need a new perception of 'national security'. This cannot come from existing ministries – each looks out on the world according to its own departmental perspective. The new Ministry would create a new perception based on an annual review called the National Security Assessment (NSA).

The NSA would cover such assessments as: defence, disarmament, the nation's work within international organizations such as the UN, energy, the international protection of human rights, and assistance to developing countries (including financial aid and terms of trade). The central questions it would address each year are: what is the state of the nation's national security? How does this assessment compare with last year's assessment? Has the international security situation improved or deteriorated? What should be done to meet the challenges posed by the international security situation?

The new Ministry would also absorb the existing arrangements for disarmament matters. These would all include their negotiation with other departments which are affected, such as defence and treasury.

This would provide a unified approach to disarmament. This has to be done outside the ministry of foreign affairs. If disarmament is part of a ministry of foreign affairs, then all disarmament considerations will be viewed within the context of wider foreign policy issues, for example, the need not to offend allies while also missing no opportunity to criticize less friendly nations. Instead of disarmament being seen as an important objective in its own right, it will always be subservient to other considerations, some of which may be adding to international tensions. When disarmament considerations come first, we acknowledge our global responsibilities.

'Peacebuilding' is the economic and social task designed to remove the deep-seated causes of conflict. Peacemakers can negotiate agreements to keep combatants apart, but as long as international suffering and inequalities exist, there will be a need for peacebuilding.

The challenge of peacebuilding is to be tackled at two levels. The more obvious task consists of a nation's various programmes in which assistance is given to people overseas, such as the provision of foreign aid, the relaxation of trade barriers and help for refugees. All these tasks could be co-ordinated by the new Ministry.

Secondly, there is the management of interdependence. National governments find increasing difficulty in solving their problems on their own since there are so many factors outside their control. Transnational problems require transnational solutions. The possible 'greenhouse effect', the hole in the ozone layer, acid rain, and marine pollution all require international co-operation. The new Ministry would handle a government's co-ordinated approach to global interdependence.

To conclude, the end of the Cold War presents us with a new era. The old techniques for settling disputes are of little use – if we persist in using them, then the window of opportunity presented by the Cold War's ending will be replaced by a continuation of some form of the old warfare state. The 21st century requires a new way of looking at how we handle conflict. Conflict resolution is a more creative response than relying on warfare.

War is a dying business. The challenge is now to make conflict resolution a growth industry.

OUR SHARED RESPONSIBILITY FOR FUTURE DEMOCRACY

Vaclav Havel

And as for the future? . . . If a contemporary scientist thinks at all of what will be in two hundred years, he does so solely as a personally disinterested observer . . . And a modern politician? He has absolutely no reason to care, especially if it might interfere with his chances in an election, as long as he lives in a country where there are elections. . . .

It is my opinion that the dramatic developments of the past few years, the past few months and the past few weeks have added a special significance to the fact that deliberations on culture and democracy are to take place now in this part of the world, in one of the countries that have freed themselves of totalitarian rule and set out to build democracy.

What is it that has happened in this part of the world? What is going on here?

It started with Gorbachev's perestroika in the Soviet Union which implied that the communist power in the USSR, or the more progressive forces of that power, began to realise the depth of the moral, political, social and economic crisis which decades of totalitarian system had inflicted upon the whole society. Perestroika – an attempt to carry out a radical reform of the system – has paved the way for processes which it probably did not originally envisage. Truly democratic political forces began to emerge in the Soviet Union and its peoples and republics started to shed the bondage imposed upon them by the centralist power. Then came the democratic revolutions in the countries of Central and Eastern Europe, the downfall of the Berlin Wall and the German unification and then, finally, this grand movement has culminated in the democratic revolution in the Soviet Union itself which was triggered by the abortive attempt at a coup. That attempt, as it turns out, was probably the last spasm in the death agony of the totalitarian system, the last major action aimed at saving it.

We can say that the totalitarian system in the whole former Soviet bloc is now in ruins. Until recently, there were a First, a Second and a Third World. The term 'Second World' is now losing its previous content, maybe it is becoming devoid of sense altogether. What is left thereafter is a vast complex of ruins and debris, and an open space combining features of the First and Third Worlds: with its aspirations and its desire to build a democratic political system and a working and prosperous market economy it is turning toward, and seeking to rise to the level of, the First World which it would wish to join; with the present state of its economy and the kind of nationality-based and social problems it is facing it resembles rather the Third World in a number of ways.

It seems that the world as a whole, and in particular what has been called the First World, has been somewhat taken unawares by such a dramatic and rapid disintegration of the Second World which it had come to describe summarily as communism. For years the First World used to criticise it, confront its expansion, support all strivings for observance of human rights and democracy there. At the same time, however, it was quietly growing accustomed to its existence and adjusting itself to it. Now, it is a little bit surprised, a little bit confused, a little bit bewildered as these major changes are compelling it to abandon fast its own patterns of being and stereotypes it has adhered to so far and to ask itself an absolutely fundamental question: how to deal with the fact that the 'evil empire' whose existence has helped it until now in its own self-identification is now disappearing from the Earth? The First World has learned to live with it, next to it, in opposition to it, it has become used to that way of life. Now it finds itself in a situation where it has to do something it has desired, but ceased to expect to happen – that is, to live without it. The so-called Third World has no less of a problem with the new global situation: it, too, to some extent has got used to being just the third, a domain of rivalry between the first two, and now has to ask itself what this change means for it and how it should cope therewith.

Obviously, there is no need for me to stress that the disintegration of the Second World is bringing the whole planet a great hope – a hope of an end to the bipolar tensions which used to encircle it so tragically, and of an end to the mad arms race, a hope of a tremendous enlargement and thus of a considerable deepening of the space where reason, freedom, democracy, pluralism, justice and humanism pre-vail, or at least have a chance to prevail.

However, this disintegration also entails – what good would it be to ignore that? – as yet a number of potential risks. A number of undiscovered mines are still hidden in this vast area of ruins and debris which people and nations are now seeking to remove in an effort soon to build something better. The danger of a variety of nationality-based, ethnic, political and social conflicts, as well as of economic crises, of chauvinism, intolerance and clashes of hundreds of special interests is substantial throughout this area. We are seeing it now in Yugoslavia, tomorrow it can happen anywhere else in the post-communist world. While communism may have been to a Western democrat an alien, repulsive and to some extent unintelligible phenomenon, he has already got to know something about it, has learned to handle it and to estimate its reactions and possible courses of conduct. What has remained after the fall of communism may worry him anew, and in a way maybe more, because of its new quality and new inscrutability: communism was static, unchanging time came to a standstill whenever it ruled. The terrain emerging after its collapse is dynamic, full of change, with time galloping by leaps and bounds, and it is difficult immediately to adjust to such speed.

If the civilized world does not want to just watch and tremble, to think what may yet happen here, if it wants to boost all the hopes which these changes are bringing nearer and suppress all the dangers hidden therein, there is only one thing it can do, and that is to do, without waiting and without indifference, everything in its power – in the interest of all humankind – so that the situation in this part of the world, too, may be stabilized soon.

This means among other things – and perhaps first of all – to give generous support to everything that is related, and conducive to democracy and its culture. The culture of free and responsible citizenship and of political dialogue, furtherance of models of truly democratic behaviour and building of truly democratic institutions and rules – these are the best instruments for countering irrationality, intolerance, political adventurism, short-circuit-like actions, chaos, inscrutability, that is, the most threatening dangers that are now making themselves felt on the ruins of communism.

I believe that all genuine democrats should now do something towards this end. The great hope that is opening before all of us at present must be fulfilled. Those of us making an effort to remove the debris left in our part of the world by the era of communism cannot be left at the mercy of fate. It is not only economic investment that we are asking for. We also urgently need investment in our political culture.

EVERYONE HAS THE RIGHT TO PARTICIPATE IN CREATING THE FUTURE

Kjell Dahle

'New ideas give inspiration to action. When historical leaps have taken place it was often as the result of a synthesis between contemporary reality and visions of the future.'

The idea of futures studies implies the 'colonisation' of the future by experts and specialists. New 'high priests' may create 'scientific' images of the future, which make ordinary people even more passive than before (Galtung 1971).

This is negative, and not just from a democratic point of view. Future policies may be decided by a small elite, but they still have to be implemented by all of us in our everyday lives, As a result, as many people as possible need to be inspired and empowered to participate in futures studies.

Futures studies thus need a political and a democratic element. But it will not do just to ask people what they want, for instance in the form of social surveys. Even researchers using surveys as a method, see the weaknesses of them; as Ornauer points out:

> 'They may tell us something about what is in people's minds, very little about what is in the back of their minds or deep down in their subconsciousness, and nothing (or next to nothing) about structural relations not reflected in their consciousness at all.' (Ornauer 1986.)

Neither is it sufficient just bringing people together, and seeing what happens. If we are to meet the challenge of declining positive images of the future, there are two main challenges for participatory futures studies, namely to find processes and structures that help bring out the best of our imaginative potential as individuals, and secondly to build a foundation for creative dialogues between different individuals and groups.

When it comes to *our imaginative potential as individuals*, serious reflection about what kind of future we prefer has interesting effects. Basing his conclusions on experience from futures workshops, Richard Slaughter describes the effects as follows –

> 'When the nature of those wants, or needs, is reflected on with clarity (rather than simply assumed in a commonsensical way which merely reinforces the status quo), visioning becomes a precursor of social and cultural innovation.' (Slaughter 1991.)

Deeper reflection makes most of us end up with quite different-looking futures from those we participate in creating by our economic behaviour in the market or those futures that come out as a sum of our answers to opinion polls.

Imagining desirable futures as individuals is, however, one thing, active participation with the aim of shaping alternative futures is more demanding, and different forms of *creative futures dialogues* are needed. Futures workshops, combining critique, fantasy and implementation, is one way of inspiring and enabling people to create visions (Jungk 1989). Problem solving communities where groups of researchers meet politicians, bureaucrats, business people and representatives of other groups is another. A 'problem-solving community' meets to formulate research programmes or to 'arbitrate' between researchers and other groups.

Creating the necessary dialogue between scientists and other groups to be involved in the participatory studies is, however, not an easy task. The character of this challenge can be best understood if we take a look at the communication problems within the academic world itself, especially when it comes to interdisciplinary research. Including non-academic groups does not make the task any easier. (Dahle 1991/92). In fact, the competence most needed within participatory futures studies is not specialists with qualifications within any particular field of knowledge, but the ability to encourage dialogue between people with different kinds of background. i.e. Generalists who can apply the knowledge of different specialists within a wider context.

The Swedish sociologist Mats Friberg from the University of Gothenburg has addressed this issue. He has developed a methodology that combines the need for political action and creativity with scientific demands for truth and systematics. His VETA methodology which contains four intertwined elements: (Friberg 1986):

VISION: to test one's evaluations and create visions of possible and desirable futures.

EMPIRICISM: to describe the development of society until the present.

THEORY: to explain this development and predict probable changes under different conditions.

ACTION: to participate in the formulation of a desirable future.

In the VETA-model, the arts are involved because of the inclusion of visions. The element of action brings in the need for a constructive dialogue between scientists and politicians, planners or grassroot movements.

Linking all the four elements of the VETA model, and working with them at the same time, is an enormous challenge compared with methodologies within ordinary research work. Such methodologies are limited to the interaction between theory construction (T) and empirical research (E).

Futures studies aims to solve problems. The limitations of scientific methodologies encouraged Friberg to question whether science is a part of the solution or a part of the problem. Researchers are, however, not the only group with a narrow framework. Politics tend to concentrate mainly on the interaction between Visions (V) and Action (A). Sometimes even the visions can be rather invisible when it comes to power-seeking party politicians.

Application of the VETA-model can help concerned scientists, who are lucky enough to operate within a framework where their skills can be used in a relevant way for society. It can also help parties and organisations create more knowledge-based visions.

THE ALTERNATIVE FUTURE PROJECT – A NORWEGIAN ATTEMPT

The state-funded Norwegian Alternative Future Project, gives an interesting example of a Scandinavian participatory futures study. The project is based on a dialogue between researchers and social movements, and it has tried to combine the four elements of the VETA methodology.

The aim of the Alternative Future Project has been to arouse the widest possible interest in the development of society according to alternative guidelines, through active democratic choice. This goal is to be achieved by solving three main tasks:

★ The development of one or more knowledge-based models of an alternative society based on the values of the Alternative Future Project, giving higher priority to social goals and responsibility for natural resources and the environment than to material and economic affluence.

★ The analysis of how free we are to reorient the course of development towards an alternative model of society, the situation in the Nordic countries being the object of study.

★ The promotion of the first steps to be taken towards a desired future society, by trying out some alternative ideas and assessing whether they are workable in an overall concept.

The idea of a Nordic Alternative Future Project arose at the end of the 1970s. Driving forces behind the concept were the Norwegian Society for the Conservation of Nature and a social movement called The Future in Our Hands, led by the author Erik Dammann. (Dammann 1979)

Allied with 15 other non-governmental organisations, these two movements recognised that on their own they could not provide the knowledge needed to realize their ambitious project. They therefore wanted an independent study, in which various forms of professional expertise could collaborate. In this way, the movements hoped that their visions could gradually move towards reality.

Such hopes for the future were not only found in the NGOs. Many Norwegian politicians also wanted another kind of social development, but found this difficult to achieve on a timescale reaching only to the next parliamentary elections.

An appeal in support of the project collected 30 000 signatures in our country of 4 million inhabitants, and was supported by a great many prominent people in different sectors of society. For instance, the presidents or vice-presidents of the majority of the Norwegian Federation of Trade Unions signed, as did 7 of the 10 bishops.

A clear majority in the Storting (Norwegian parliament), including all parties except the Conservative Party and the right-wing Party of Progress, decided to finance a preliminary project. In 1985, the main project started, having at its disposal about £ 500 000 each year. The board has, until recently, consisted of representatives of the special council of researchers supporting the project, the group of NGOs who took the initiative, and the staff. The diversity within the Alternative Future Project has thus been an example of what we called a 'problem-solving community'.

Major projects completed or nearing completion include a collection of studies on social disintegration in modern society, an investigation of the Norwegian population's attitudes to the value system underlying the project, a project on feminist images of the future (Halsaa 1988), a book on popular social values in a region of Norway, social experiments in the Nordic countries, alternative Nordic energy scenarios and the relationship between free trade and the social and ecological values on which the project is based. The project has also developed a computer database of ideas called '*In Practice*' containing information on social and ecological experiments which are in line with the values of the project, and played an important role in the international NGO activities connected with the report of the UN World Commission on Environment and Development (Hille 1990).

The expectations of the project have been very high and on this basis it can hardly be considered a success so far. During 1991, the project was more or less taken over by the Norwegian Research Council for Science and the Humanities. A new director has declared in public that the idea of positive utopias is 'dead like a stone'. Towards the end of the year, the staff demanded that the project should be split in two. Former staff members and members of the board have now established a new futures studies institution called 'The Ideas Bank'.

The Alternative Future Project, illustrates the risks such projects run of being swallowed up either by the traditional science system or by the day-to-day problems of politicians or grass-root activists. (Dahle 1991/92.)

However, in spite of its shortcomings, the project has shown what can be done, in that important parts of the power elite now recognize the long term social and ecological problems connected with the present world order. Probably for the first time, the political authorities in a western society are funding a project with the explicit aim of shaping alternatives to the existing political and economic system.

THE FUTURE OF THE MIDDLE EAST

By H.R.H. Crown Prince El- Hassan Bin Talal of Jordan

'There is a tide in the affairs of men
Which, taken at the flood, leads on to fortune;
Omitted, all the voyage of their life
Is bound in shallows and in miseries.
On such a full sea we are now afloat . . . '
– William Shakespeare, Julius Caesar IV:3

The Middle East is presently at a crossroads in its history. These times may be viewed by our children of the next century as an era when the region finally began to move towards establishing the conditions for sustainable peace and justice for all alike. Or they may see these as days presaged by yet more false dawns, days when we wasted our opportunities, squandered our chances. We pray that history may judge in favour of the former; but we know that there is much work yet to be done if we are to succeed.

The pace of progress towards peace is such that comments on the Middle East peace process are likely to be superseded by events between the time of writing and publication. In my chapter, I would therefore like to present some ideas that are gaining credence in the Middle East, particularly in Jordan. We believe that there is more to peace than the absence of conflict, that the no-war, no-peace stasis that has ruled too long in the Middle East ultimately serves the interests of none of the parties. We believe that these new ideas are capable of facilitating that vital breakthrough for which we all pray, and laying the groundwork for a dynamic, creative and mutually enriching peace for the 21st century and beyond.

A new thinking is beginning to emerge in the Middle East. It sees the interconnections and interdependence between peoples, while respecting their diversity. It holds cooperation and communication to be the keys to the future. It knows that no one perspective has a monopoly on the truth, and that solutions to any problem must address the whole of that problem, not merely its most troublesome symptoms. This thinking therefore comes from a broad inter-disciplinary basis, and seeks a concept to govern the region that goes beyond the immediate crises of any given moment.

An examination of the history of the Middle East reveals that conflicts over resources, demography and ideology have traditionally been met militarily. Of all aspects of security, it has been the military dimension that has held precedence, at great human cost. It is becoming increasingly apparent that this military dimension of security is incapable of furnishing lasting solutions satisfactory to all.

The most obvious example of the hegemony of the military paradigm concerns territory. In the Gulf alone there have been no fewer than twenty-two active border disputes since 1900, all dealt with by military means. This has in turn fuelled military spending, leading to massive debts as eager suppliers of arms compete for customers. The inter-relation between energy, arms and debt is plain to see in this context. It is an enduring and telling irony that the five permanent members of the UN Security Council, empowered to uphold peace around the world, together account for approximately 90 per cent of the world's arms trade. This over-emphasis on the military dimension, together with great and growing economic disparities in the Middle East, has given rise to what may be termed the political economy of despair.

Similarly, if it is clear that there are great disparities in the region, the nature of the challenge for the future is equally clear. We are facing the most far-reaching task of our history as we move into the 21st century. The threat of apocalyptic war between two nuclear superpowers has receded, and democratisation and global respect for human rights are on the ascendant. But these developments, though encouraging, are not in themselves a guarantee of a peaceful and sustainable future. On consideration of H.G. Wells' dictum that 'human history is in essence a history of ideas', it becomes clear that we have yet to replace the ideological antagonism of the Cold War with a new reference system based on universal values and consensus.

A new framework of thought has yet to be created to carry us safely into the future we all seek.

Issues such as resources, the environment, refugees and arms control are by their very nature trans-national, and must therefore be addressed collectively. This includes not only the regional players, but the international community at large. For any one player to attempt to exert military, political or economic hegemony in the region can only lead to stultification throughout the region, and the perpetuation of the material disparities that currently fuel the political economy of despair.

We in Jordan therefore seek to take a new approach: we regard multilateral negotiations and security and cooperation arrangements on regional issues to be of paramount importance. This is an innovative, even ambitious, approach; but a brief parallel with developments in Europe will serve to illustrate why we believe it to be the only model with a chance of ultimate success. Europe, like the Middle East, was plagued by war and internal rivalry for centuries. It is now proceeding down the path of integration and cooperation; Europe has reached the level of development at which traditional enemies such as France and Germany view themselves more as partners than as adversaries. A similar process now seems to be evolving independently among the ASEAN group of South-East Asian countries. Jordan shares the confidence of these regions, which have experienced similar historical processes, in the Conference on Security and Cooperation.

But although an idea may be the driving force of history, it can be of little benefit if practical applications cannot be found for it. The regional Conference on Security and Cooperation lends itself well to such application. I mentioned border disputes earlier as an example of an area in which the military dimension of security has traditionally been the means of settlement. In such cases, we would favour peaceful negotiation with ultimate recourse to the International Court of Justice, and the implementation of a Regional Environmental Plan. To take another example, rather than dealing with the scarce resource of water by fighting wars, we advocate a Regional Water Plan administered by a representative Regional Water Authority to ensure fair distribution of this vital resource to all. Proposals for a Regional Development Fund, a Debt Sinking Fund and a Regional Development and Reconstruction Bank have already been made. A regional Agency to regulate and supervise arms control – both conventional and weapons of mass destruction – is also badly needed.

In essence, then, our vision is of a Middle Eastern Helsinki process: a fully fledged Conference on Security and Cooperation for the

Middle East. We believe that such a model can eliminate the political economy of despair. Democratisation, freedom of expression, human rights and greater awareness of and reliance on the political, legal and economic dimensions of security provide a route towards the alternative political economy of peace, security and progress: a sustainable future.

The participation of states with a similar experience in conflict resolution, peace-keeping and regional cooperation is of course imperative to assist the countries of the Middle East in overcoming their difficulties. In this respect at least, the Middle East idiom needs to be globalised. New security arrangements must by their nature link up with those of neighbouring regions; in the case of the Middle East, Europe in particular. So while a new forum based around the Mediterranean region is the immediate objective, thinking on yet a wider scale is required in the long run, for when it comes to the issues that truly affect the course of mankind's history, we are all neighbours on this Earth, North and South, East and West together. No one is immune to the dangers posed by weapons of mass destruction, environmental abuse, and the mass-scale demographic movements that accompany political, cultural and economic despair. The only conceivable way that such issues can effectively be addressed, is together.

We are aware that this vision requires the laying aside of dogma, of prejudice, of traditional hostilities. In the Victorian age, a time not dissimilar to our own in many ways, John Stuart Mill wrote of the need to re-examine continuously our assumptions and our beliefs, to subject them to the most rigorous scrutiny. We too, at the end of the 20th century, must learn to reconsider our prejudices and learn tolerance for different ideologies. All ideologies have certain common points, together with their differences. We must develop the breadth of vision to identify and build upon these common points, while remaining firm in our demand that every government respect those rights of human beings set forth in the Universal Declaration, and fulfil the universal requirements for health, food and purpose for all, irrespective of nationality, religion, gender or ideological inclination.

These requirements and rights, like so many of the challenges of today's world, go beyond questions of national strategy or ideological labels. They form the starting point of a humane discourse that appreciates the common ground and moves towards a constructive dialogue. Growing awareness of the ecological paradigm across the world is a cause for much optimism. We feel that this may in turn lead us to a paradigm in which the human person is restored as the proper focus of politics and economics: a new 'anthro-politics' for the 21st century and beyond. Various proposals, including the implementation of a Human Charter, have been put forward to this end. We find in their substance much to consider, and much yet to be done, if the world is to develop into the place we wish our children to inherit. For they will inherit it together, as one, and so will have little patience with antiquated protestations of regional strategic considerations and rivalries.

Our efforts in the Middle East must therefore be placed squarely in the context of the developments in the rest of the world. As we move into the new millennium, certain changes in social, economic and political practice are already becoming apparent. Growing awareness of the need for sustainability in areas of policy ranging from population to energy has given rise to a more forward-looking paradigm than previously. Issues of development are beginning to be looked at more from the perspective of partnership than aid. There is a noticeably growing perception that mankind must choose the long term framework over the egotistic and politically opportunistic short term approach. The power of human needs, both material and non-material, is being seen across the world to be ultimately more enduring than military might. Perhaps more than anything, this last development is cause for optimism.

There are, however, inherent contradictions in the emerging world order still to overcome. To take but one example, simultaneous developments have been discernible towards greater homogenisation within regions of the world on the one hand, and a rising tide of ethnicity, in terms of small communities taking pride in their language, culture and identities, on the other. It seems, paradoxically, as if we are at once moving towards broader and narrower frames of references. We in Jordan believe that the key to a successful future is to strive for unity in diversity, and not vice versa. The infinite combinations and enrichment possible in a world no longer polarised, the benefits available from unprecedented access to the heritage and wisdom of all cultures of all times, make any other credo unthinkable for a future that is to live up to the promise of the human race.

In such a future, the challenges of regions and the world as a whole will be met by the peoples of the world not as adversaries but as partners, despite the many tragedies that mark all our histories. The Middle East is an area that has borne more tragedies than most, and that might appear to have inherited a more insoluble conflict than any. Perhaps for that reason, a special onus rests on my region to show the rest of the world what can be done when true peace is the intention of nations. If progress can be made towards a peaceful, sustainable and equitable future in the Middle East, one might conclude that the same is possible anywhere; that no conflict, no matter how apparently intractable, cannot be resolved. For our endeavours to succeed, we will need not only to overcome the barriers that divide the sides in the conflict, but to call on all the resources and experience of the international community at large to help place us firmly on the path to the 21st century. We believe that such a process is now occurring in the Middle East, and that ideas of the kind outlined in my chapter can do much to bring about the goals we all seek. We are pledged to do our utmost towards those goals, for we know that should we fail, we would condemn the children of the next century to an unsustainable future, to shallows and miseries of our own making. But if we succeed, we hope that they will look back on these times with wonder, and give thanks that we had wisdom enough to seize this flood tide of opportunity in the Middle East.

BUSINESS TO THE RESCUE

Francis Kinsman

*'Those who forget the past are condemned to repeat it; but those who
anticipate the future are empowered to create it.'*

'Bliss was it in that dawn to be alive!' Wordsworth may have meant it
at the time, but can we honestly feel that about ourselves today? We
huddle in front of the TV, glued to catastrophe after catastrophe. The
ethnic implosion of eastern Europe; the shattered bodies of Belfast,
Beirut, Soweto . . . ; the gasping environment; the sobbing children;
and yet another suave politician with his weasel-wimp snake-oil
remedies. And what do we say to each other? 'Pass me another After
Eight, please, dear'.

And yet.

Something Else Is Going On. That Something could just be the first
faint glimmer of tomorrow – the first day of the rest of the life of the
human species – that dawn. The vision I postulate here is nothing less
than the most exciting period of human history ever, the most
dangerous, the most imperative, the most awesome harvest imagin-
able, the razor's edge between salvation and annihilation. That possible bliss.

There is not much time, however. If my analysis proves too
optimistic, and the light at the end of the tunnel turns out to be
another train thundering down on the same track in the opposite
direction, then as a species, we will exit promptly and leave our planet

to the dolphins who will undoubtedly make a much better, though more watery job of it over the next 50 million years or so. For our part, we now have only about fifty years to get it right in; maximum one hundred.

It is arguable here that Homo sapiens has been programmed with a serious design fault. Sapiens, meaning wise, is just what we are not; clever, or possibly cunning, is more like it. As T.S. Eliot laments, 'where is the wisdom we have lost in knowledge; where is the knowledge we have lost in information?' Too much left-brain/technological/number-crunching/logical stuff, and not enough of the fey, intuitive, creative, feeling, lucky, right-brain bit. That is the root of our current problem.

So having made such a shambles of the story so far, is there a chance that we can write a happy ending to it? Only through wisdom; a sobering consideration. But astonishingly, breathtakingly, there does appear to be a gathering of the collective consciousness, a gigantic leviathan heaving itself up out of the sea, a critical mass of motivated thought that seems to be attuned to the Something Else, that dawn itself.

The irony is that the power that could appear to be pulling us out of our icy darkness is an evolved model of the original creature that virtually drowned us in it in the first place. That is to say, business, with all its inherent defects.

You can forget governments because they are too unwieldy and short-term. Forget individuals because they are too weak and short-term. Forget impassioned movements because they are too undisciplined and short-term. Instead, think about business if you are in any way thinking about a force we can harness to extract us from the current mire. And this we need.

The economist/philosopher Adam Smith wrote of the 'unseen hand' of the market. The market has recently come into a lot of flak because, post-Thatcher/Reagan it is now politically, incorrectly seen as a mechanism for grinding the individual into the dust. In reality, this criticism should be angled towards the largely 'imperfect' markets of today's capitalism, which are admittedly oligopolistic, rigged and in restraint of genuine trade.

Instead, a new 21st century breed of capitalism with an ethical stance is what we must design in their place; based on the 'perfect markets' that Adam Smith originally envisaged. Ever been to a market? Sussed out the best value bananas from among the stalls? Of course you have; and that is what Smith meant was crucial – wide choice and absolute information for all the punters.

Believe it or not, this is very definitely on today's menu now. The information is increasingly there for the asking, given our new technology; and so is the diversity, given our increased internationalism. All we have to do is to seek and choose, as consumers, as investors, as employees, as associates, as pensioners, as Jane and Joe Public. It is so simple. Nobody ever said it would be *easy*, but *simple* it certainly is. Business is there for the taking; and for the making. It is entirely up to us to insist that it does well by doing good.

Today's motto for business success is beginning to be recognised as 'people matter most'. So what we have to do is to challenge that principle, and to complain like hell if we get the wrong answer, in every personal capacity. The difficulty? We have to will to do so; and that, as with every ethical decision, is up to every one of us, voting with our feet. Business is poised to listen. It has never been more sensitive to demand. The present demands on it, which are up to us to voice? For there to be –

* a keen identification by employees with the organisation's distinct and positive mission, and an integration of their work and their personal lives, embracing their own personal development in a working context;

* an active relationship between the owners/shareholders and the business itself – preferably involving as many as possible of the employees;

* honesty and integrity in all decisions and information, paying bills on time, honouring contracts in spirit as well as in letter, treating the customer with respect and dignity;

* providing a product or a service which is relevant and socially responsible, involving activities that are not only harmless but preferably beneficial to the community and to the planet, either directly or indirectly.

We humans are both brilliant and impossible, both animals and angels. But in an immediate sense, we do have the muscle to act out our various parts in the marketplace. In this capacity, if we are to survive at all, we must create and manifest a code of decent dealing, of cooperation as well as the natural urge to compete.

300 years before Wordsworth, de Montaigne wrote that 'there is . . . no state so bad that provided it has age and stability on its side, it is not preferable to change and disturbance'. Silly old devil, he got it wrong, even though in the same breath he also admirably said that 'one must always be booted and spurred and ready to go' (de

Montaigne) Change is inherent now, and we must accept it and ride it like a surfer rides the waves.

So meanwhile, somewhat after Wordsworth, Darwin's dictum, 'survival of the fittest' can now be re-stated as 'adapt or die', as far as the human race is concerned. And business is the key to it: a different and more humane kind of business. That is tomorrow's reality.

With good fortune our grandchildren may look back when they are old, and sigh, 'Bliss was it in that dawn to be alive . . . ' May they enjoy a host of golden daffodils in tomorrow's brilliant spring. But it is up to us to ensure that they do so. As put by Arthur K Watson, until recently President of IBM –

> 'Providence was not whimsical when it chose business to bring the world together. People care about business; they may never agree about religion or ideology but there is a logic to business, and through it we may see this quarrelsome, troubled world brought together.'

CHANGE, TRENDS, UNCERTAINTIES

Wolfgang Michalski and Michel Andrieu

Over the last 30 years or so major changes have taken place in the world economy. What broad sweep changes can be expected in the future? While this question cannot be answered credibly in terms of a forecast, it is nevertheless possible to examine the principal geo-structural changes likely to shape the evolution of the world economy over the next decade or so, notably the parallel trends towards increased internationalisation and regional integration and the changing patterns of international competition; to identify some of the main driving forces which underlie these trends, such as trade and investment, technology, and environmental constraints; and to reflect on some of the uncertainties and major risks decision makers will have to face in the years ahead, notably geopolitical changes and the related threat of increased protectionism, the possibility of global imbalances between saving and investment as well as regional uncertainties and risks of conflicts.

MAIN GEO-STRUCTURAL CHANGES

Projections for the global economy in the 1990s and beyond are by and large optimistic. In the industrialised countries, after more than a decade of widespread restructuring, conditions on the supply side are favourable, and provided international financial markets remain stable, the recovery in investment rates over the latter half of the 1980s should feed through into improved output performance over the longer term. Moreover, private consumption and investment could pick up in the debt-stricken developing countries, as well as in Eastern Europe. Thus, estimates for average annual growth in world output up to the year 2000 are broadly in the 3% range. North America and OECD Europe are seen as likely to grow at between 2.5 and 3%, Asia at well over 5.5% (slightly higher for the Asian Newly Industrialised Economies), Latin America at around 3%, and Africa somewhat lower. For Central and Eastern European countries, great uncertainty still surrounds growth rates for the next decade.

A major continuing trend will be the growing internationalisation of economic activities. While this process was largely determined in the past by increases in world trade and more recently by the globalisation of international financial markets, it will increasingly be fuelled in the future by international investment and corporate coope- ration in the development and application of new technologies. Growing internationalisation will lead to increasing interdependence between nations and a correspondingly reduced ability of individual governments to pursue independent policies. At the same time, the regional integration already under way in Europe, in North America and – to a lesser extent – in the Asia-Pacific region will intensify. While some form of loose economic co-operative economic arrange- ments may emerge in Asia, none of the foreseeable solutions can be expected to match the European or North American set-up in terms of effective political weight or international bargaining power.

Competitive pressures will force a gradual shift of labour intensive activities from advanced economies to lower cost countries, notably in Asia where a gradual relocation of industry is occurring from Japan and the most advanced NIEs such as South Korea, Taiwan, Hong Kong and Singapore to the second tier NIEs. However, as the ability to respond rapidly to changing market conditions becomes increas- ingly important, firms will have a growing tendency to locate at least part of their productive facilities close to markets. To the extent that the determinants of competitiveness will be found more and more in man-made comparative advantages and in structural features of domestic economies, governments will need to pay increasing atten- tion to maintaining a stable macro-economic environment, well functioning product, capital and labour markets, a well trained labour force and efficient productive infrastructure.

KEY UNDERLYING FACTORS

While the major structural changes which are shaping the evolution of the world economy result from the subtle interplay of a wide range of factors, some of these such as trade, investment, technology and ideological shifts appear more relevant than others both in terms of their impact and of the direction of the causal relationship. Global environmental constraints, although they do not contribute directly to change, can be considered as another key factor since they represent an increasingly powerful indirect influence which will force a substantial reassessment of policies and practices in a wide range of areas.

In the future, trade flows and investment flows are likely to continue to grow rapidly and to become increasingly related as intra-industry and intra-firm trade increases and as a growing number of companies become truly international or even multi-domestic. Technology, notably progress in Information Technology, new materials and biotechnology will have implications which will go far beyond the economic sphere, extending to all facets of society. While industrialised countries will be best placed to exploit the new technologies, industrialising countries will have to forge technological links with OECD firms and be themselves prepared to devote increasing resources to research activities.

Environmental constraints, notably the greenhouse effect, will force a reassessment of the use of fossil fuels worldwide. While OECD countries will have to bear the largest burden of CO_2 abatement, they cannot do it alone and international mechanisms will have to be established to ensure an effective and equitable sharing of the burden. Finally, one of the most important factors likely to influence the future evolution of the world is the change in attitude which is taking place in a growing number of countries, with higher value being attached to individual efforts and initiative and to the capacity to adjust to change. At the same time, there appears to be an increasing recognition of the limits of government intervention in the economy.

UNCERTAINTIES AND RISKS

While increasing internationalisation and interdependence as described above do contribute to economic growth and to a more effective allocation of worldwide resources, they also represent a major source of uncertainties as individual economic agents as well as governments become increasingly exposed to a complex interplay of market forces and other processes over which they have less and less control. Three specific risks stand out as particularly important. The first one relates to the future evolution of international economic relations in a world economy where the relative geopolitical positions of the key players (United States, Europe and Japan) will continue to change; the second pertains to the future evolution of the balance between global investment needs and world saving; and a third type of risk may arise from the instability of regions which are particularly important for the future of the world such as the Commonwealth of Independent States and the Middle East.

In the absence of an effective set of internationally agreed new rules of the game, for instance in such areas as competition, investment and technology, the evolution of the world economy towards tri-polarity could be unstable and result in trade conflicts detrimental not only to the countries involved but even more so to Third World countries. In particular, the NIEs such as Korea, which pursue export-oriented growth strategies and are still highly dependent on technology inflows from the advanced countries are bound to be caught in the cross fire. A growing ex ante imbalance between saving and invest-ment at the world level is another risk factor, one which could result in substantially higher interest rates to the detriment of growth, notably in developing countries, and result in a further widening of the welfare gap between the First and the Third World.

Because of particularly explosive combinations of political, econo-mic, cultural, religious, ethnic and social factors, often exacerbated by rapid population growth which will put increasing strain on resources, a number of countries and regions of the world have become increasingly unstable and could be the theatre of serious conflicts in the future. While some of these conflicts are likely to remain purely local or regional others, in particular such as may erupt in the Commonwealth of Independent States and the Middle East, may have worldwide implications, including heightened risks of nuclear proliferation and increased migratory pressures.

To cope with the challenges and to seize the opportunities of the 1990s, not only OECD countries and the dynamic Asian economies including Korea but also the rest of the world will need a stable and open international environment in the years ahead. A successful completion of the Uruguay Round and a strengthening of interna-tional co-operation across a broad range of economic and other policies could contribute to such an environment. As key players in international discussions, the United States, the European Commu-nity and Japan can and should also significantly contribute to shaping the environment they need. The extension of the Community and the creation of NAFTA could contribute to trade liberalisation and economic stability not only in North America and Western Europe but also in Latin America and in Eastern Europe. Closer links between Japan and other Asia-Pacific countries could liberalise econo-mic relations and foster growth in the region. This more stable and open international environment could in turn initiate a virtuous circle of growth and help to provide a more favourable context in which equity and environmental issues could be tackled in a more co-operative and more effective manner, including the problems faced by the most underdeveloped regions of the world.

THE 21ST CENTURY FROM AN ECONOMIC PERSPECTIVE

Noriko Hama

'. . . What we are witnessing now is the chaos that must surely arise when the whole world is looking for a new wineskin that is able to contain the new flow of things to come in the next century without being torn apart at the seams.'

History may have a habit of repeating itself, but it can never go back or stand still. Similar sets of circumstances may provoke similar responses and it is possible as well as legitimate if well researched, to draw parallels between something that occured a hundred years ago and what unfolds in the contemporary world. In a play, especially if not very well written, the hero may find himself in act two facing very much the same sort of plight that befell him in act one. Nevertheless act two is act two and the action has progressed in the meantime. On the stage of economic history, we have come a long way from the earlier acts of barter trade to the current one of financial wizardry and high-tech. Whether we are any the wiser for it all is of course another matter; still, the fact remains that we have evolved. History is essentially and inherently about change.

One may argue that the degree of change abates with time. The learning curve flattens as we glow older, and the law of diminishing returns sets in. One may ask: will the 21st century look as radically different from the 20th century, as the 20th does from the 19th as we know it? The answer, insofar as economics is concerned, is that rarely has the momentum for change been greater. 20th century institutions, notably those that were established in the latter half of the century, have become so disjointed that the creaks and clangs are all but audible.

It has to be said that the whole form and nature of the global framework as shaped by the 20th century, whether it be in terms of geopolitics, international relations, or economic management, is facing inexorable overhaul. Small wonder that the president of the United States has to seek a new world order, though more pressing matters seem to have put that quest on hold lately.

All that has gone before has essentially become ancien-régime. What we are witnessing now is the chaos that must surely arise when the whole world is looking for a new wineskin that is able to contain the new flow of things to come in the next century without being torn apart at the seams.

Many occurrences point to the declining ability of 20th century systems to hold things together. Among the most significant incidents in this regard have been the collapse of the Soviet Union, the reunification of Germany, widespread eruption of ethnic conflict throughout eastern Europe, the credit crunch in the United States, and the financial bubble and its subsequent puncture in Japan. The 20th century way of doing things simply does not seem to be working any more.

What then, lies at the heart of the 20th century way of doing things? This question has to be answered before a vision of the 21st can emerge. The question is obviously not a simple one and probably deserves a very complex answer. Yet complex answers are never very interesting and for the most part not very enlightening either. So, at the risk of being taken to task for over-simplification, here is a two-word answer: management and control.

That these were the key words in the communist world is a truism and needs no elaboration. It may draw more debate to say that the capitalist system has also operated largely under the rules of management and control. For all the talk of free markets, the period in which market forces held full sway was really not a very long one. It would be nearer the truth to say that much of the time since the 1940s has been spent in trying to control and contain those very forces which were supposedly the hallmark of free market economies.

Depressions were so abhorred and full-employment became so overwhelmingly important a policy and political preoccupation that demand was never allowed to fall below supply. Financial instability came to be considered such a dangerous thing that interest rates as well as the activity of credit institutions in general became the object of rigorous regulation in many economies. Events earlier in the century led policy makers to regard finance as an animal best kept behind bars; to allow it to run rampant would lure companies and individuals into dangerous indiscretions and eventual bankruptcy, and economies into great depressions. With demand management as protection against job loss and regulation to keep financial crises at bay, it was thought that a disaster-proof system had been created to provide lasting prosperity.

Yet cyclical fluctuation and financial volatility were in fact valuable adjustment processes through which capitalist economies could maintain longer term equilibrium and resilience. Deprived of these outlets through which inflationary gases could be suctioned out of the system, imbalances within an economy were apt to become so pronounced that the ultimate pain in correcting them would be a lot more damaging and harmful than it would otherwise have been. That financial regulation has been progressively relaxed once more over the latter decades of the century in many countries is itself an indication that the pressures mounting from never ending demand expansion had become too great to bear. Something had to give. While the desire to guard the nation against hardship is both an understandable and admirable policy sentiment, too much management and control can nonetheless lead to distortions that bring ultimate vulnerability, if not demise. The plights of the U.S. and Japanese economies cited earlier are graphic illustrations to this effect; more on this later.

Trade is another aspect of the free market system that has not been free over the years. True, the GATT was created as a body whose task was to liberate trade from protectionist barriers and arrangements. But it was nonetheless an attempt at institutionalising trade. That the elimination of obstacles against the free flow of goods, and more recently services remains the GATT's fundamental mission is without dispute. Yet the very pursuit of this mission does by nature involve intervention and the attempt to manage and control the way in which trade is conducted. As in the case of finance, trade also became too dangerous an animal to be allowed to run wild. Chains were needed to keep it in check. After the dark days of protectionist trading blocks that proliferated through the 1930s, this again was a perfectly legitimate concern. Still, the fact is that there is not all that much room for market forces to determine the manner in which trade is conducted these days.

In fairness it must be said that the GATT is not to blame for the many arrangements, bilateral for the most part, which exist today that keep trade in certain products in chains. Many such arrangements stand between the United States and Japan, in clear violation of the GATT's fundamental ideals of multilateralism and non-discrimination. While the GATT regulates for the sake of freedom, as it were, these arrangements directly aim to restrict trade flows between the signatory nations.

If we may accept that management and control have been the governing concepts of the 20th century economy, and that that way of doing things is working no more, it must follow that the coming century needs to discard those concepts and go in another direction. If control is not working, the solution is not more control but less of it. This seems largely to be the direction in which the world is actually heading. The communist economies have made a clear decision to go that way. The capitalist economies are, interestingly enough, more ambivalent.

Indeed they are not so much ambivalent as reluctant to give up the accustomed ways. What is happening as we head toward the turn of the century seems to be a conflict between the underlying market forces which groan for freedom and the policies of containment. This tug of war is what lies at the bottom of the recurring stock market collapses that we began to experience in the late 1980s. In the end, the effort to manage and control may prove self-defeating. There are limits to which corrective forces can be contained when macroeconomic equilibrium is seriously undermined. To persevere regardless may lead to an eruption that is all the more powerful and damaging for having been repressed so long.

Readers will no doubt recall that stock markets were visited by a nasty jolt over the third weekend of November 1991. New York went down by 120 points, the Nikkei subsequently lost just a little less than 700 points. While the thin ice sustaining world financial markets did not shatter into bits as a result, the moment was nonetheless a frightening one.

Enough has seemingly been said about the causes of and the circumstances leading to the would-be crash of November 1991. The general feeling is one of a collective sigh of relief that the wolf failed to do much harm, even though the cry of its coming was not a false one this time. Yet has enough indeed been said and has the wolf really lost the power to harm? The more logical answer would seem to be that the wolf is a tenacious animal, it is invariably harmful and that while it may shy away on one occasion, it can always come back, so long as there is reason to do so.

Not to put too fine a point on it, the United States economy was in a very serious mess at the time. It was thought to have bounced out of recession some months before. Had that actually been the case, that fact in itself would have posed dangerous problems of premature overheating. Subsequently it became apparent that no amount of cajoling or bullying could get it on its feet again. President Bush's exasperated call for lower credit card interest rates, which were seen as the direct cause of the stock market plunge, sounded very much like the cry of a man on the verge of a nervous breakdown.

The U.S. malaise is deep rooted but not necessarily complex; it suffers from gout. The only cure for that particular illness is stoicism and frugality. In this sense, the economy's refusal to respond to monetary stimulus, and perhaps more significantly, the banking system's inability to diffuse the stimulative effects were the economy's own defences against the further corrosion of its well being. It was beginning to say no to excessive management and control; It wanted to have its own way.

It therefore came as no surprise that the President's prescription of a further easing of money met with such a violent rejection from the stock market. The doctors were in danger of the ultimate folly. In the attempt to ease the painful symptoms, they were endangering the patient's hope of survival. This fundamental error of judgement is what makes stock markets plunge repeatedly; in 1987, 1989, 1991, and probably again, soon.

The significance lies not in the fact that such plunges have not led to all out disaster, but that they keep happening. To the extent that the gouty man will not relent, the pain will keep returning, until something snaps. Interest rates are already unjustifiably low in the United States, but given the policy psychology of the moment, the government may actually demand yet more cuts. This may prove to be just a little too much for the banking sector to handle in terms of profitability. Alternatively, it may lead to a perverse shrinkage of lending.

The recession needs to work its way through in the U.S. economy, to a point where the macroeconomic balance begins to show signs of correcting itself. The balance of payments did at one point appear to be heading in that direction. No sooner had it done so, policy began the attempt to steer the economy away from that particular turning. Management and control once more.

The advent of Paul Volcker's stringent monetarism in 1979 presented a crucial opportunity for the U.S. economy to rid itself of its unhealthy habits. The cure proved too painful and the policy was dropped prematurely. More than a decade later, nothing has changed, except that the sickness has sunk its teeth deeper into the economy and the symptoms are growing more apparent. In the early 1980s, stock market collapses were the stuff of which nightmares were made. Nightmares of either the weak, or the uninitiated, depending on your particular perspective. Now they have become a reality, which reoccurs not infrequently.

While the United States has much to answer for in regard to the difficulties confronting the world economy today, it is by no means the only culprit. Japan and Germany are just as much to blame, though their contribution to the problem may be more recent compared to the essentially twenty year old one of the United States.

Looking back over the last decade, one wonders why Japan was ever renowned for its thrift and diligence. The great monetary thaw that began in the early 1980s has left behind it an economy whose demand has so outstripped its supply capabilities that recessions no longer have the stabilising effect that they were meant to have in the past.

Another way of putting it, would be to say that the degree of demand shrinkage needed for a return to equilibrium is so large that policy simply is not prepared to face the consequences. On the other hand, the attempt to stem the demand shrinkage is always fraught with the danger of taxing supply capacity too severely, thereby rekindling inflation. Such is the no-win situation that the 1980s have burdened us with. There can be no Keynesian way out of this state of affairs; a cause for concern, given the very emphatically Keynesian prime minister whom the country now has in the person of Kiichi Miyazawa.

Moreover, the Japanese economy shares the United States' woes in that easing the monetary reins cannot really work, because the financial sector lacks the flexibility to respond. Having played a major role in creating the bubble, financial institutions are now struggling to keep afloat in its aftermath. They are in no mood and in no position to accomodate substantive credit expansion.

Indeed the sole outcome of continuing monetary relaxation may be to steer funds out of the banking sector and into higher yielding instruments such as postal savings, which now enjoy a widening interest rate differential over bank deposits. Many will note the varying ways in which financial deregulation can cause disintermediation, but learning this interesting lesson does not particularly help the economy at this stage. The single most important lesson to be learned is that stock market collapses are not to be cheered over because they were endured, but to be heeded as important warning signals, especially as they began to hit us at increasingly shorter intervals.

Thus, there are signs that the managed system of the 20th century is beginning to give in to the pressures resisting it. The 21st century may actually be the time period in which the free market manifests itself in its truest shape, released from the chains of management. Managed capitalism will give way to market forces in their full glory.

Such a development should in turn, lead to another departure from the 20th century manner of things. This is to say that, where integration and growing interdependence among national economies had been the trend thus far, the 21st century is likely to see increasing disintegration and the dismantling of existing ties. This may seem a strange statement to make at a time when members of the European Community are about to embark on the final stretch of their marathon towards full economic and political integration. Yet observe what has happened in the now defunct Soviet Union. One could not ask for a more potent piece of evidence that loss of central control leads rapidly to disintegration. A great deal of management and control is needed to hold varying national economies together.

Now that the dismantling of the Soviet Union is complete, the divisive tensions will become yet more severe as well as complex. Severe because the issue of economic self-sufficiency and the command over productive resources will come more prominently into play. Complex because these concerns will become interlaced with the problems of national boundaries that cut through ethnic groupings. The tensions are already becoming apparent.

The irony is that this whole situation which is now unfolding within what used to be the Soviet Union serves as vivid proof of the essential legitimacy of perestroika as a theory of economic reform. Its failure is blamed for the collapse of the union and not unjustly so. Yet this current mounting of tensions among the republics, notably between Russia and elsewhere is the very situation which the original scenario for reform had hoped to prevent. To the extent that nations seek rigid self-sufficiency, the fight over resources is ultimately unavoidable.

It is only in the context of a greater entity that economies can serve as complementary elements to each other. And it is certainly difficult to make this happen of the participating nations' own accord. This is the problem inherent in what is known as complementary or vertical integration among national economies, that is to say the integration of economies where one nation has in abundance a resource or resources that the other finds scarce within its own borders. What this entails is the pooling of resources and the sharing of a common supply. Without central control and management, this is a lost cause.

With the centre in control, there was at least a fair chance of retaining the complementary relationship among the economies of the republics. Take away the centripetal force, and it will become very difficult to hold the pieces together. In the extreme instance, serious conflict could arise as republics seek to gain control over precious resources. When such economic causes become superimposed over the quest for independent ethnic identity, the situation cannot be treated casually.

Members of the European Community clearly cannot remain aloof from these currents blowing in their neighbouring regions. Indeed given the situation one has to ask if a deepening of the community of the twelve can remain a relevant objective. Yet the further away it moves from this goal, the less significance the community will have as a process toward economic union transcending national boundaries.

In their summit meeting held in Maastricht in December 1991, the twelve EC members agreed to aim for greater political integration and the completion of an economic and monetary union (EMU) with a single European currency by January 1999. Britain and Denmark retain the option of not joining the currency union, but this does not detract from the significance of an explicit commitment to aim for a single currency regime.

The Maastricht Treaty is the culmination of a year long intergovernmental debate on the twin issues of political and economic/monetary integration. From a historical perspective, the debate itself was the final stage in a process that has been in the making since the signing of the Treaty of Rome back in 1957. As such, it comes as no surprise that the agreements have the appearance of a comprehensive and well thought out document, for all that the ambiguities are many and the cohesive force is tenuous.

Yet there is every reason to question the viability of the blueprint drawn at Maastricht. Notably in terms of the economic and monetary union process, the agreements assume a laboratory like situation in which the far-reaching changes taking place in eastern Europe, the crumbling of the Soviet empire, the closer economic ties with the Nordic countries, and even the fact of a unified Germany are essentially ignored. The code word that opens up the way toward monetary union is economic convergence of a quite stringent kind, and yet everything that is happening around and within the European Community speaks loudly of greater divergence.

The freer manifestation of market forces and resulting disintegration will inevitably lead to chaos. One is always inclined to envision the future as a more orderly place than the present, but perhaps this too is a 20th century trait. Chaos is by no means a bad thing. There is great energy for growth and change embedded in chaos; after all the world was created out of chaos. From it can spring much that is creative. The 20th century's obsession with productive excellence and expansion has in many ways steered the human race away from creativity. This is perhaps most applicable to Japan, especially in its earlier post-war history. Mass productivity became the all-consuming objective. By contrast, the 21st century could become the era of mass creativity.

It will undoubtedly be a very difficult world to cope with. The new world order that the United States and others are seeking may turn out to be a total absence of order. And why not? Better that, surely, than risk being stifled to death by the 20th century mechanisms of control, which if they are to have effect, will have to be applied with ever greater force. Perhaps the earlier statement that history does not go back will have to be contradicted. What we are about to do in the 21st century may be to go back into the melting pot of creation.

A VISION OF UNIVERSAL EDUCATION

Malcolm Skilbeck[†]

> '. . . *visions of better futures, whether in health, environment, human relations, urban life or that great intangible 'the quality of life' . . . requires as a necessary condition of their realisation, improved education.*'

The twenty-first century will be the century of universal education, for all people, worldwide and throughout their lives. This vision, first entertained by the Moravian bishop, Comenuis, the year of whose death 300 years ago is being widely celebrated in Europe in 1992, has taken several centuries to mature. After this long gestation, both its feasibility and its necessity are now apparent.

Visions are one thing. The ways to their realisation are something else again. Often these ways do not exist or cannot be created or, when they are created, ironically serve to frustrate the very dream that gave them birth. The rise and now the fall of the classless communitarian ideal under Marxist-Lenist communism is a timely reminder of how the methods devised to implement the sought-for ends can ultimately both defeat the ends and bring them into disrepute.

There are many other examples of the decline or collapse of utopias and idealism under the weight of inertia, opportunitism or muddled thinking about how to reach the desired goal. Yet, the post-Enlightenment belief in the possibility of ... indeed the necessity for human and social progress ... continues to spawn visions of better futures, whether in health, environment, human relations, urban life or that

† The views expressed are the author's own, not necessarily those of his employer, the Organisation for Economic Co-operation and Development.

great intangible, the 'quality of life'. It is a common feature of the optimistic scenarios in these and other spheres of human endeavour that they require, as a necessary condition of their realisation, improved education.

A lesson of history, then, is that in considering visions we must pay careful attention to procedures, methods, principles of action, to ensure that they further rather than frustrate our ends. At present, our principal, but not our only ways of achieving the vision of universal education are the institutions – schools, colleges, universities – and the formal programmes of study for which they are responsible. None of them is perfect. Indeed, some would argue, echoing Mark Twain's advice 'not to let schooling stand in the way of your son's education', that the institutions too often generate failure and frustration to be regarded as satisfactory vehicles of a truly universal education. Since it is these very institutions, which, during the past couple of centuries have made education so widely available, criticism of their shortcomings must be tempered by a realisation of the triumph of civilisation and human culture that they represent, their shortcomings notwithstanding.

The adoption of policies of compulsory and free, i.e. state-provided, schooling for all and the legislative and financial frameworks established through these policies have been, in the nineteenth and twentieth centuries, a dramatic step forward in human welfare.

It is now becoming evident however, that the model of state-provided state-controlled schooling for all has severe limitations which can be overcome only by taking a wider, more flexible and more creative view of the educational process itself and its place in our social lives. The industrially advanced, stable democracies of the Organisation for Economic Co-operation and Development have moved rapidly, since the 1960s, towards the universalisation of secondary schooling – on the basis of universalisation of primary schooling which had been widely achieved by the time of the Second World War. During the past thirty years, these societies have also substantially expanded provision of post secondary, further and higher education, to the point where it is, in several countries, at the stage of or on the verge of being a mass phenomenon, with a third to a half or more of the relevant age group participating.

But, for a variety of reasons, this quantitative expansion is unlikely to continue on its present trajectory of 'more of much of the same'. The vision of universal education will not necessitate the abandonment of present thinking and practice so much as reconceptualising and recontextualising. This means getting our educational policies as it were into a new key. Sceptics will question the need as well as our ability to do much about structures and processes that are now so well embedded in the life of the modern state. But sceptics usually suffer from a narrowness of vision that prevents them from seeing anything except what is directly in front of them.

Consider the problems education in its present form is facing. Significant numbers of students are not succeeding in school, college and university, are dropping out and seeking other avenues for their energies. It is questionable whether the regime of full-time, institutionally based education can be made appropriate to the needs and interests of the whole population. The corollary, however, is not the acceptance of less than a universalist philosophy, but rather the need to find alternative means that have a greater likelihood of attaining the sought-for ends. A second difficulty arises from the role the state has traditionally assumed – the role of provider and controller. We are coming to the end of the era in which the concept of the 'public interest' in education is best served by the elaborate, cumbersome and costly machinery of ever multiplying state structures and state institutions. The reason is not only cost, although that is a major consideration. More fundamentally, it has to do with the evolution of our ideas about the proper spheres of action: for the state, for communities, enterprises, professional bodies and individuals. The state has a legitimate interest in the outcomes of education – for example in the society-wide diffusion of civic values and basic skills and the servicing of industry, commerce and the professions with highly skilled and well-educated personnel. This should not be confused, however, with the continued role of the state as the owner and operator of schools, colleges, also in many countries of universities, the arbiter of curricular details and the employer of teachers.

There is already evidence, notably in the traditionally highly centralised education systems of the European continent, of a radically changing and frequently diminishing role of the central state apparatus. Paradoxically, in several of the Anglo-Saxon countries which have traditionally favoured a highly decentralised pattern and a plurality of mechanisms for control and governance of the institutions, governments of a generally right wing tendency have moved to assert greater state control. In Britain, for example, the establishment of a national curriculum for schools reverses a long-standing trend towards devolved responsibility. Similarly, in the United States and Australia, national targets are being set for core subjects in the curriculum.

While these apparent counter-moves represent a significant reversal of non-interventionist policies by national governments they are nevertheless consistent with the thesis that the longer-term tendency is towards a greatly lessened role for central government in the direct control and management of the institutions themselves. Government interest even in the Anglo-Saxon countries can be expected to shift increasingly towards a goal – and outcomes – rather than a detailed management approach.

These, then, are two of the principal considerations that lead to the conclusion that the universalisation of education in the twenty-first century will not simply be an extrapolation of present structures and mechanisms. There is a third, which is the design, testing and development in recent years of systems of education which constitute a radical challenge to the publicly provided and controlled schooling model. This third factor is an amalgam of a number of ideas and movements: self-paced instruction, independent learning, experimental and distance education and open learning. Mainly, but not exclusively in the domains of post-compulsory schooling, further and higher education there are now quite workable models which make the vision of universal education attainable. The two central ideas are that learning can be, within broad limits, self-paced and that instead of the learners going to the institutions, the institutions go to the learner.

In higher education, open or distance education universities throughout Europe the Americas, South Eastern Asia, Africa and Australasia are now producing hundreds of thousands of graduates every year who have completed all or the larger part of their studies never having attended the institutions, and through contacts that might include correspondence materials, regionally-based workshops, summer schools, telephone tutorials and computer hook-ups. Commonplace existing technology, of which the two key components are high quality, low cost printing and an efficient postal system has made possible the dramatic expansion worldwide, of higher education at a distance. The next stage – already well under way – is to extend this to all or practically all subject areas including technical and professional subjects such as engineering, health care, computing, agricultural and fisheries management, etc. and to make vastly increased use of the technology of the personal computer.

Despite prejudice and a 'closed shop' mentality which continues to operate in many technical and professional areas, distance higher education has moved well beyond the humanities and social sciences where the study requirements, being mainly linguistic and literary, can be readily met by traditional correspondence courses. What is necessary is to combine the resources of the specialist distance education providers with those of the more conventional institutions so that the former get the benefit of the concentration of knowledge and expertise found for example in traditional universities, while the latter make increasing use of distance education designs and technologies for example in their part-time undergraduate courses and for part-time graduate students.

It is said that emphasis on distance education and individualised self instruction is only for adults – younger students need all that 'the school' stands for by way of structure, direction, supervision and, indeed, compulsion. In the first place, the dichotomy between mature and immature students is overdrawn; there is scope for greater autonomy and wider choice in school level education. But, in the second place, the very problems schools face in achieving appropriate learning outcomes for all students must give a pause to think about ways of modifying, reforming and even restructuring schools themselves. It is of little avail if we oblige everyone to attend school and then fail to educate significant numbers.

The question of the most appropriate technology for universal education is being addressed, but thus far on too limited and piecemeal a basis. We need to be eclectic on this point, treating technology as a set of tools, which the knowledgeable performer, whether student or teacher will draw upon with discrimination and in accordance with the task in hand. Accepting the point that students themselves will increasingly make a financial contribution towards their own education and training, a much greater consumer orientation is to be expected. The most expensive educational technologies are not necessarily the best and, as cost becomes increasingly a consideration for the consumer, the level of costs will be a definite factor in consumers' choice. Printed text will undoubtedly remain a major vehicle of instruction and learning due to its universality as a medium of knowledge, its low cost, its portability and (for teachers) its user friendliness. But print has its limitations: it is of only modest flexibility in interactive learning where, as in a tutorial, a dialogue of statement, comment, question and answer is desirable: moreover, print is not a substitute for direct experience where observation, demonstration and practice of a technique or skill are needed. The classical models of the tutorial in the classroom and demonstration lessons in the laboratory have provided for these interactions, but they, too, have their limitations. For example, they do not readily admit of self-paced learning, they usually require a rigidity of timetabling, not all students thrive under them – and they are too costly as a basic mode of universal education.

THE INTELLIGENCE REVOLUTION REVISITED

Geoff Woodling

Conventional wisdom is the judgement reached by the majority of those concerned with a given matter after a long period of debate. . . . It is therefore a compromise, out of date and embodies a powerful interest in surpressing challenge.

The closing decade of the millennium produced a wealth of futures, although few had trusted the earlier imaginings of science fiction. Predictably, the shock of unfolding events in Europe overwhelmed the more enduring patterns of change. For many, the end of communism was seen to herald the end of the global balance of terror. Few cared to recall that before the events of 1989 had signalled the end of communism in eastern Europe, attention had been focussed on the bicentennial of 1789. A poignant conjunction of events, where 200 years earlier Britain stood back from the Jacobean chaos to relish the weakening of French power only to find herself fighting the resurgent forces of empire a few years later. No-one seemed to consider that a Russia freed from the shackles of Soviet Empire might become a new menace – except those in China. That is where we now know communism finally met its Waterloo in the successful Tibet rebellion, fuelled by an Indo–Russian alliance against China.

In the late twentieth century, writings of futures now past (and surprisingly most were still committed to paper text, at a time of emerging hypermedia), there was a presumption of the supremacy of capitalism. It was widely acknowledged that the failure of Marxism had shorn the 'underprivileged', or to be blunt, the desperately poor, oppressed people of the world of any defence against the future excesses of government-protected capitalism. The *Financial Times*

proclaimed the *Death of Marxism* in its final leader of 1991, and
expressed the complacent view that there was no 'case for a revival of
some of the fire and passion of Marxism in order to give the poor the
dignity of struggle and the rich of the earth the smell of a bit of fear'.
No case for Marxism perhaps, but supreme complacency to find no
place for fire and passion, let alone dignity and fear.

Such passions were soon to be fuelled in the East by the resentment
of the new economic protectorate established by the European Community. The future had appeared safe beneath the commanding
heights of capitalism. The obvious failure of the Soviet command
economy had not alerted the West to the progressive almost inexorable subversion of the capitalist system by governments everywhere.
The tinkering with privatisation had deceived many into thinking
that government involvement in the economy was on the wane. Such
a long view of the future was perhaps inevitably distorted by its
perspective from the commanding heights of the developed world.
This reflected a long held preoccupation with 'top down' thinking in
societies at the time. Of course, those who attain the highest position
are rewarded with an opportunity to see further, the sense which
humans value most. However, the distortions of perspective infected
their view of the future. Vision had become one of the qualities
expected of those in power – a quality which promised much and
meant little.

For many, the ascent of the commanding heights had become a
lifelong commitment to a redundant metaphor from the age of
artillery. In the era of the smart missile which broke on the world in
the Gulf War of 1991, concealment and stealth, long the trademarks
of the guerilla, were to become the new model of effective
organisation.

The future was no longer a top down view. Gradually it became
possible to recognise the forces which shaped the potential for change
at lower levels of society. The technology and practice of intelligence
gathering revolutionised the mapping process. The collection and
integration of multiple data sources and their representation in multi-
dimensional imagery began to reveal new understanding of the
processes of change upon which there had been so much speculation.
The 'Intelligence Revolution', as we now call it, removed the distortion of distance. It captured information from beyond the threshold
of our senses. It challenged to the foundation the system of organisation in which the energy to accumulate knowledge had vested power
in the commanding heights. The future from the bottom up became a
legitimate concern and not just for those with the fire and passion of
discredited theories.

The practice of exploring the future from the bottom up had been developed by a small group of individuals who founded the Business Futures Network in the 1980s. The initiative had its origin in Stanford Research Institute's scanning process which provided early warning of change from a Californian perspective. Adopting the same process, but extending it to a group of individuals in widely different roles in diverse sectors and countries, the network developed an informal source of global early warning intelligence. It was a precursor of the kind of intelligence networks which began to develop in the aftermath of the demise of the CIA and KGB. The Intelligence Revolution came about once organisations recognised that their most critical assets were trustworthy sources of information and that it was of critical importance to find ways to harness their potential. Of course, such a 'revolution' did not occur top down. It subverted the levers of power through the networks of informal communication. Its impact was to change profoundly the way organisations managed their activities. It also enabled people from the bottom to acquire the knowledge to challenge authority.

This future had been anticipated in one Forum of the early Business Futures Network which concerned itself in late 1990 with the issue of 'the quality of information' and the increasing vulnerability of organisations which overlooked this concern. At the time, there had been little attempt to link the notion of quality to the provision of information.

The quality of information was a new frontier. The capacity to create enormous flows of information was beginning to debase its currency. Being able to detect when a source is misrepresented, misquoted or found to be unreliable was to become an increasing requirement in many fields of activity. The doubt cast on scientific papers reporting questionable experimental evidence may have been newsworthy, but was almost certainly minor by the standards of commercial disinformation. The difficulty of evaluating corporate financial health was only part of the picture. Claims of sales, orders, product breakthroughs, had become the stock-in-trade of so many journalists and journals that their value was totally undermined.

Six months later, the Forum considered in greater depth the vulnerability of the banking system to the misrepresentation of evidence used in the preparation of credit ratings. The lack of any effective standards for credit rating did not deter people from placing great faith in the product. Banks were soon to be both victims and villains. Within months, the early signs of collapsing confidence in the world financial regulatory system had accompanied the discovery of fraud on an enormous scale in Tokyo, New York and London.

At the time, few organisations had begun to use scientific methods in the use of information for business decision making. The emergence of the scientific enterprise was not a reference to research, but to the testing of business hypotheses in the classical observation – deduction – testing procedures of science.

It only required a small shock to trigger the loss of confidence in the financial information markets. An early signal had been the false market in Maxwell Communications Corporation, whereby threats of legal redress had prevented normal market information systems from carrying commentary then spread by word of mouth. This was a further sign that investors no longer had trust in the regulation of financial organisations. The ensuing collapse of confidence hit hardest at the nerve centre of the capitalist system. The lack of accountability created opportunities for profit in disinformation. It was compounded by the discovery that systematic computer fraud had been perpetrated on the foreign exchanges. The movies of the period created a new heroine from the Global Fraud Squad and ex-head of MI6, no longer indicting spies, but seeking to confront new criminal syndicates.

By that time, as anticipated earlier at a BFN Forum in San Francisco in 1991, concern was rising among those who felt governments were unable or unwilling to protect their wealth and freedom. Computer hackers' fear of government harassment led to the formation of the 'Electronic Frontier Foundation' – for debate on computer security and privacy issues. Such organisations exerted influence through the media. The media then became important sources of community power. They reflected the bias of the constituents they represented. Media networks came to be thought of as organisations representing the interests of their customers (local TV distribution), advertisers and stakeholders. Sensationalism and trivialisation sold newspapers: objective reporting and balanced analysis did not.

However, while the notion of a free press or broadcasting service died hard, professional journalism was no longer a guarantee of objective reporting. The integrity of media reports had to be constantly checked. Grass roots media were no more objective, but created public awareness for the issues they championed. Governments had become the victim of their own isolation. In smaller communities such as Norway, it still reflected concerns at grass root level. Elsewhere, as in Japan, the bureaucracy was seen as a spending agency, where agents were not expected to take any initiative, a preserve of only its highest elite.

At the same BFN Forum, discussions about the need for organisations to improve the quality of their decision making in response to new challenges, explored opportunities in the teaching business.

By a strange coincidence, this was to be the development which began to challenge the competence of government on a wider level. In the UK, a decision had earlier been taken to privatise the Schools Inspectorate. This was widely held at the time to have been misguided. The creation of the new private sector agency took longer than expected, not least because no-one really knew what schools would pay. Soon afterwards, an enterprising Italian media entrepreneur, familiar with innovations in Italian schools, acquired the new business. He had recognised that popular concern to ensure higher standards of education meant people would pay to know which schools or local authorities provided the highest quality of service. It had the effect of introducing competition into the supply of education almost overnight. The business has now been acquired by the new World Teaching Corp which franchises its methods to community schools around the world.

This was the first awakening of the then new concern for quality of service. It was to comprise the second element of the attack on government. Already the vulnerability of government had been exposed by the appallingly low quality of information on its own performance and hence its inability to provide an acceptable level of service. For most of the next ten years, the administrative bureaucracies fought a rearguard action to preserve their monopoly of power. They were, however, fatally weakened in their resolve by a third force.

The triviality of much administrative work in these organisations had created disaffected, low quality workforces, unwilling and unable to take any initiative in response to the challenge they collectively faced. This was an issue that had long remained overlooked, while commentators puzzled over the declining productivity of the information workforce. The issue first surfaced, somewhat surprisingly, in Japan. That country began to experience a labour shortage earlier than America or Europe, because it could no longer rely on the migration of young workers from rural areas to the Tokyo-Kansai metropolitan region. This began to expose companies to wage pressures from established staff, who were increasingly unwilling to undertake the menial or trivial tasks which young females, especially, had performed.

The pursuit of ever more intensive production was generating a rising need for staff to maintain the increasingly complex organisation of service in transport, health, finance, environment and so forth. The alternative to creating an immigrant or domestic underclass demanded a reappraisal of the value of work and of the way people would willingly contribute to meeting new demands. To maintain a way of life with a diminishing pool of labour but without consigning at least some of society to low value existence, was only to be possible if the value of work were not determined by price alone, but more by the intrinsic contribution it allowed the individual to make.

The problem was not confined to menial tasks, but revealed a deep dissatisfaction with the symbolic manipulation of information in a daily work routine. The apparent relief to be had from physical exertion, whether through a preference for manual labour, sport or exercise, demonstrated that symbolic activity deprived of any imaginative stimulus is an inadequate form of work. The futility of much symbolic activity represented the information equivalent of the nineteenth century factory worker chained to routine, not in search of wealth, but survival.

For the first time, people began to withdraw their willingness to work in such roles. At different times, many segments of society had chosen not to be employed. The over 55s, under 25s, privileged or wealthy women were now joined by a group who sought the freedom to choose how to spend both their time and money in demonstrating what they contributed to society. Their pay was not related to the quantity of work, although most worked very hard.

Japanese organisations began to be transformed ahead of their peers overseas. The late diffusion of information technology in that economy, combined with a chronic labour revolt, achieved a characteristicly swift restructuring. Unlike the half-hearted decentralisation of government bureaucracies elsewhere, the Japanese realised that it was a matter of survival for their society to shed labour from government and avoid the creation of an urban immigrant underclass to fill the labour gap. Faced with loss of confidence in government as elsewhere, the Japanese were fortunate in having perhaps the best educated workforce to profit from their rapidly growing intelligence resources. This they did to extend still further their famed quality of service. It was a revolution in competence which gave initiative to the front line administration rather than the elite. The empowerment of the information worker extended to a whole range of services in which it became possible to employ smarter methods to serve the needs of perhaps the most complex and dense society on earth.

The Intelligence Revolution in Japan accompanied that country's transformation into the world's first quaternary economy. When wealth created from the transfer of knowledge became the single largest contributor to the economy five years ago, it was what the Japanese themselves had predicted thirty years earlier in 1990. The transformation of government itself represented the creation of a knowledge business in recognition of the fact that in many areas of life, the market mechanism is unable to operate. This did not mean that the agencies of administration could not be challenged by private sector competition. Their role was to employ scarce people and resources to the best advantage of the communities they served. The transformation of government enabled communities to exercise far greater control over their own affairs.

This challenge was very soon felt in other areas. Communities had long bemoaned rising violence, even in Japan where it was perhaps more subtle, but no less insidious. The failure of the judicial process and the increasing expense and irrelevance of legal advice combined to induce a lack of trust in the maintenance of the rule of law. As in other spheres of government, the law was subject to both international tension and to community pressure. The enormous complexity of the legal process began to collapse under the weight of documentation. In its place, local communities created new legal service organisations, whose role was to provide the infrastructure for exercise of the judicial process within the community. In practice, this meant that each became the guardian of the legal rights and responsibilities of community citizens – a form of collective defence founded on easily accessible, logical intelligence resources.

Medicine was second only to law in its inability to provide value for money. The high priests of medicine were inaccessible, expensive and in many cases unable to comprehend the complexity of the system of which they were part. Not surprisingly, the monopoly of medical knowledge began to be challenged by organisations which could provide rapid access to sources of medical information. They soon realised that once this was combined with a medical and environmental record for each individual, it was possible to provide advice on vulnerability to illness and help people improve their lifestyle and wellbeing. The Intelligence Revolution had begun to create community health services which replaced the illness bureaucracies and, incidentally, most life insurance.

The knowledge that quickly spread the benefit of different lifestyles, contributed to changing work patterns. It also made people realise how little control they had over the savings they made for later life. The increasing awareness of responsibilities and risks of longevity made it more important to exercise judgement over those who managed personal savings. This hit life insurance companies and pension funds very hard. The abysmal investment performance of organisations lacking any commitment to their customers, and restricted in their range of investments and knowledge of new markets, soon became a target for attack. The North American experience was well ahead of other regions. The combination of legal, medical and pension costs was to exceed 30% of the per capita income in the late 1990s. The benefits were widely held to flow mainly to the suppliers of the services and not to the customers. This crisis precipitated the decision to cap the cost of all three types of services, forcing large lay offs and pressure for more cost effective service. This followed the example of cost containment in the early stages of transformation of the British Health Service. The creation of personal health contracts provided a new form of life insurance, free of legal redress, except in rare circumstances, and offering benefits for savers who maintained high personal standards of health.

The Intelligence Revolution which hastened many of these changes was of course not like 1789 or even 1989. It was more a mushrooming of experiments. At first their significance was scarcely appreciated. There was a confused call for constitutional reform, in the mistaken belief that the old system of government could be recreated for new communities. While this change was resisted by reactionary forces, they were soon overtaken by events. It had become apparent to our friends in the network as long ago as 1989 at a workshop in Warsaw, that the political power structures within society were on the wane, and that new centres of influence were emerging. The Swedish Social Democratic Government, ahead of its demise in 1991, had anxiously commissioned a large study into this issue within Sweden. As in the US, it found that new communities were beginning to secure influence through control of local media or administration. City mayors were often the new power brokers, as Moscow and St Petersburg were soon to demonstrate. The Los Angeles initiative to replace sales of the internal combustion engine after 2005 was perhaps the most influential local precedent of all.

Moscow and Los Angeles were at opposite ends of the economic spectrum. Not surprisingly, those with the least became increasingly alienated from the economic system. The model of the free market which communities, especially in regions which emerged from communism, were obliged to adopt, served only the demands on the passing global industrial system in which they had little prospect of ever competing successfully. The transformation of government became an urgent necessity if communities were to determine how to intervene in the economic system to meet local demands. Environmental management, as Los Angeles had demonstrated, was foremost among the demands which the global economic system was unable to supply. The acquisition of knowledge and application of local capital were critical to the ingredients which new organisations were to employ in the service of their communities. The regulation of local monopolies, the recycling or maintenance of products and infrastructure all became local priorities. None of this would have been possible without a revolution in the way information resources were employed and knowledge created, priced and transferred. The Intelligence Revolution permitted new administrative services to supplant old government bureaucracies. The privatisation of local government had paved the way in the UK, but was hampered by institutional constraints on community, fiscal and executive independence.

A good example of the benefit of knowledge transfer was the early sale of traffic management expertise from the UK to Japan in the late 1990s. A consortium of Birmingham City, one of the Baby Bells and a Swedish vehicle producer won the competition to provide neighbourhood traffic management systems in Tokyo. This demonstrated how communities could profit from knowledge developed to serve local needs. New groupings of people and enterprises began to address common needs and exploit market opportunities to employ their knowledge globally. Networks of individuals began to form the new arteries of trade.

This development did not occur without disruption. Worst of all, it encouraged a damaging conflict over the protection of intellectual property. This could not be resolved in the previous international trade forum known as GATT. This collapsed in 1995, as its increasing irrelevance in managing an international economy was appreciated. Physical trade had long ceased to be a useful criterion of economic wealth or independence. The value of financial transfers, services and knowledge payments replaced dependence on trade. The dematerialisation of production and replacement of mass through higher value design and performance encouraged local manufacturing. The principal conflict arose between new organisations which began to profit from selling local knowledge well ahead of older institutions of research and learning. These agents of government were often incapable of protecting know-how or of funding its commercial development. Nationalism in knowledge protection was fortunately impossible. Those organisations who prospered, recognised the need to secure resources for shared development on a timescale appropriate to the endeavour. The loss of income from earlier research was a source of trade friction which was resolved only when governments agreed to end research subsidies and hand responsibility for all 'knowledge factories' over to trading enterprises. These were to pursue protection of intellectual property with a new global organisation set up to provide a registration service.

The Intelligence Revolution was set to become the principal agent of transformation of the economic system. BFN members had pon-

dered whether the demise of capitalism would follow far behind the
death of communism. As it turned out, the failure of the commanding
heights of state planning was a signal of the collapsing confidence in
western style government. The revolution which occurred did not
replace capitalism, but secured its divorce from big government. The
economic empowerment of communities was made possible by their
acquisition of the knowledge which the Intelligence Revolution made
possible. The rapid collapse of government bureaucracy had provided
the largely unforeseen catalyst for this transformation.

BIOTECHNOLOGY AND THE CHALLENGE OF CHOICE

Philip Sadler

'Optimists and believers in progress are confident that mankind is capable of making choices that will greatly improve the quality of life for the great majority. Pessimists fear that God or nature will exact a terrible revenge for such arrogance.'

Imagine a society in which women can, if they wish, have children at the age of sixty and in which elderly people whose mental abilities are beginning to fail can have brain transplants of silicon cells and become as sharp, mentally, as eighteen year olds. Such ideas would, not so long ago, have seemed fantasies of science fiction. Yet we now accept that they will almost certainly be commonplace by the year 2020. American scientists have already built a silicon retina. They now hope to build an entire brain of silicon neurons and link the two together.

TECHNOLOGICAL PROGRESS AND SOCIAL CHANGE

Major leaps forward in economic development and major transformations of society are the consequences of the development of 'meta-technologies', defined as radical breakthroughs in knowledge which set in train a whole sequence of dependent technologies, inventions and products. To date there have been three such breakthroughs:

– in materials technology, starting around 10,000 BC with metal-working and leading on in more recent times to such innovations as plastics, man-made fibres and carbon fibres;

– in energy technology, starting in the 18th century with the steam engine and leading rapidly on to the electric motor, the internal combustion engine and the nuclear reactor;

– and in information processing, beginning with the valve-based mainframe computer, leading on to the PC and related technology – fax machines, laser printers, robotics, expert systems and so on.

Metal-working is associated with the development of agrarian economies and societies living largely a settled life in rural communities. The large scale production and consumption of energy is linked to the industrialisation of economies and the wholesale migration to large industrial conurbations. Finally, the information-processing revolution is associated with de-industrialisation and the emergence of the knowledge-intensive or information based economy, in which the most common form of economic activity is the provision of services. This in turn results in the post-industrial society in which the proportion of the population living in large cities moves into decline.

The next meta-technology arrived in 1953: genetics. Gunther S. Stent in his introduction to the 1981 edition of *The Double Helix* tells how at school he had been taught that the Renaissance began on May 29th, 1453, the day Constantinople fell to the Turks. For a while he lived with the illusion that on that very day people decided the Middle Ages were over and that it was now time to discover the arts and sciences. He goes on to say that, although he eventually came to appreciate the absurdity of such a notion, he would nevertheless maintain that the era of molecular biology began on April 25th, 1953, when two young scientists, Francis Crick and James Watson, reported the discovery of the DNA Double Helix in the journal *Nature*. This discovery has set in train, or is directly or indirectly associated with, a whole series of discoveries and innovations in the field of the human sciences.

Developments in the human biology field since the 1950s have been both rapid and significant. John Maddox, editor of *Nature* described 1991 as the 'Year of the Genome'. That is the name given to the whole collection of genes that makes up a human being. In his opinion, the techniques for telling how DNA molecules are assembled from simpler components are now highly advanced, with the consequence that to be able to specify the genetic identity of a person by the molecular structure of his or her DNA is now an attainable scientific goal. Indeed, the American government's Human Genome Project has set 1995 as the year by which it intends to complete its 'map' which will show which genes hang where on the 46 human chromosomes.

Maddox describes the pace of discovery as 'startling'. As an example he cites diabetes research. During 1991 a research group at Oxford

University was able to identify two abnormal genes in a strain of mice that suffers from a congenital disease which appears similar in all respects to human diabetes. Once the genes have been isolated and their exact constitution determined, it will be possible to look for the corresponding genes in people and thus to tell which people are predisposed to congenital diabetes. Leads of this kind are now a frequent occurrence, and in the past year genes responsible for twenty or so other diseases have been found.

There can be no doubt, therefore, about the nature of the new meta-technology. Clearly it is biotechnology. The difficult questions relate to the implications for the kind of society which will develop. Social change is reflected in four aspects of society – social structure, social institutions, lifestyles and values. The implications for all four will need to be considered in relation to the following kinds of developments, each one of which has enormous potential for bringing about social change.

★ More effective and less harmful drugs for the treatment of serious medical conditions and disturbed mental and emotional states.

★ Knowledge about the impact on the human system of components of traditional diets, of smoking, of alcohol consumption and of noxious substances in the environment.

★ Knowledge about the 'genetic code' making it possible first to predict and subsequently to influence such things as the sex of a child or the likelihood of congenital malformation or disease.

★ Surgical technologies making possible the prolongation of life through organic transplants or the implantation of inorganic organ substitutes.

★ Improved birth control techniques.

★ Hormone replacement therapy, delaying the onset of the menopause.

★ Genetic fingerprinting.

★ Techniques for increasing the yield and improving the nutritional value of crops and livestock.

GENETICS AND SOCIETY

The 1991 Reith lectures of the British Broadcasting Corporation were given by the distinguished geneticist Dr. Steve Jones. (Jones 1991) In the final lecture of the series he looked at the choices ahead as genetic science increasingly offers the possibility of making choices rather than leaving things to take their natural course. It is a nice coincidence that Dr. Jones works in a laboratory at University College London that was founded by Francis Galton who not only initiated the serious scientific study of human genetics with his book *Hereditary Genius*, but was also a passionate believer in the power of genetic science to improve human society.

Galton started the Eugenics movement, the aim of which was 'to check the birthrate of the unfit and improve the race by furthering the productivity of the fit by early marriages of the best stock'. (Galton 1909)

The idea was taken seriously in both scientific and political circles. In the United States some 25,000 people were sterilised to prevent them from passing feeblemindedness or criminality on to future generations. It was its adoption as a main plank of Hitler's Nazi party, however, which destroyed the movement's respectability and credibility.

Today, however, and increasingly as we move into the 21st century we shall be armed with more and more powerful tools of genetic engineering. We have to face up to the fact that we can, indeed, carry out an effective Eugenics programme if that is what we wish. Dr. Jones claims – with a complacency that I do not share – that 'no serious scientist has the slightest interest in producing a genetically planned society.' Even if this were so, what matters more than what scientists want is what the politicians want and what society wants.

The thin edge of the wedge is likely to be gene therapy. This involves compensating for a specific genetic defect by imparting to the body cells of the affected person the normal version of the abnormal gene. The unresolved question, however, is who determines what constitutes a defective gene? Although we may readily accept that the gene which predisposes to diabetes is defective and replaceable, what about genes which are discovered to relate to less universally desirable characteristics, such as skin colour or small breasts?

Issues of this kind will force through the development of a whole series of statements of values and related legislation to be adopted by societies facing conflicting demands, on the one hand for the fullest possible exploitation of the new knowledge and on the other for leaving things the way God or nature intended. There is a parallel in the current divisions within American society on the question of abortion.

GROWING OLD GRACEFULLY – THE BATTLE AGAINST AGEING

In addition to the enormous possibilities opened up by the power to change genetic inheritance, another powerful force for social change will result from the extension of the human active life-span and the defeat of many of the natural ageing processes.

The large number of old people is already a cause for concern in the developed countries, where governments are worried that a smaller working population may not be able to sustain the growth of expenditure on the health and welfare of the elderly. In Germany and Switzerland over one fifth of the population is expected to be over 65 by the year 2010. Such worries may well diminish if it appears that old people are going to need less care in the traditional sense, due to the elimination of many of the causes of physical or mental senility.

Without a doubt market forces will ensure that much of the research and development effort is directed to this purpose. What can be more attractive as a way of spending money in late middle age than the prospect of holding on to one's health, mobility and – for many people most important of all – one's sexual potency and attractiveness. This trend is already evident in the interest in such diverse offerings as hormone replacement therapy, cosmetic surgery, organ transplants, hip replacements and hopeful doses of Royal Jelly.

The relevant technologies fall into two groups. On the one hand there are those, like heart transplants, which fall under the broad, heading of 'spare part surgery'. The main likely development here is that in the future the implants and spare parts will be increasingly man-made, thus reducing dependence on donors and opening up mass markets, as is already the case with hip joint replacements, the level of demand for which constantly outruns the resources of the British National Health Service. Of greater significance, however, will be developments like hormone replacement therapy which retard or even reverse aspects of the natural ageing process, thus delaying the need for surgery or even avoiding it altogether. In the longer term, genetic screening may eliminate many of the diseases such as diabetes and arthritis which are responsible for much of the disability occurring late in life.

Traditionally the picture we have of old age is one of physical enfeeblement and mental senility – a pitiful process of reversion to an infantile state and a condition of dependence. As such the aged individual becomes a burden, an encumbrance, something of little personal worth. In recent times the practice has grown of herding these tottering relics together in geriatric 'homes' in which, at least for the less well off, conditions leave a great deal to be desired. The cost of caring for people whom medical science is capable of keeping alive, but incapable of rendering fit to look after themselves, has been a burden which, both individually and collectively, their offspring have found hard to support.

Looking ahead to the 21st century, however, we can see a very different scenario – one in which people between the ages of 65 and 85 remain pretty well as active, physically and mentally, as people in their 50s today. The majority may well not only be capable of looking after themselves quite satisfactorily – indeed this will increasingly be taken for granted – but will be able to continue to follow their occupations if they so wish, to play a wide range of games and sports, to travel extensively, and generally to lead very full lives.

We can expect large scale changes in social structure in particular regions where the active elderly population will become relatively concentrated. We can also expect wholesale changes in the lifestyles of the elderly. The possible range of lifestyles will be influenced to a considerable degree by level of income. Those with good occupational pensions, or who remain in gainful employment, will lead a very full life, particularly as there will be relatively few demands on their income from things like school fees and mortgage interest. Those dependent on state pensions and other forms of income support will of necessity lead more restricted lives, but may choose to migrate to places where the cost of living is lower and be able to enjoy a much richer life than has been the case up to now.

Some aspects of the future lifestyles of the mass of modestly affluent elderly can be seen already in places like Florida, the French Riviera and other locations serving as 'God's waiting rooms' for the relatively rich. By the early years of the next century the numbers taking up either permanent or winter seasonal residence in regions with benign climates will have grown to massive proportions, transforming local economies and, indeed, changing the balance of a regional economy such as that of Europe as a whole, bringing greater prosperity to southern areas and increasingly creating relatively deserted and derelict areas in the more northern parts.

Once in place, these septuagenarian settlers will spend their time chiefly in the less physically robust pastimes – golf, tennis, swimming bridge and cocktails. A whole range of service industries will grow up around them – in health care, dentistry, beautification, leisure activities, real estate etc. For the more serious-minded the concept of the 'University of the Third Age' will have considerable appeal and new institutions of higher education for the elderly will spring into being.

The idea of 'Grey Power' is already a familiar one, reflecting both the growing concentration of wealth in the hands of the elderly and their increasing political significance as increasing numbers coincide with a growing realisation of common interests in such policies as the defeat of inflation, the maintenance of law and order and, of course, increasing pensions. We can also expect to see the birth of new political institutions concerned with furthering the interests of this age group. All that is needed to make this a real force on the political scene is leadership.

THE CHALLENGE OF CHOICE

The really big change, however, is one so profound in its implications that trying to predict its consequences for human society defies the imagination. It is the change from a human condition which in the past has been regarded as given – by God, by nature or by random mutation, according to different schools of thought – to a human condition which increasingly reflects the choices which human beings make for themselves. Optimists and believers in progress are confident that mankind is capable of making choices which will greatly improve the quality of life for the great majority. Pessimists fear that God or nature will exact a terrible revenge for such arrogance.

WHEN THE PENDULUM COMES TO REST

Ziauddin Sardar

'Post modernism is the desert where people are prospecting for a new form of existence. . . .'

I am sitting in 'Dèlifrance' enjoying a really good cup of cappuccino. On the floor below, and I can see them clearly from where I sit, a group of Chinese maidens (petite, red silk dresses) move in slow motion, performing a classical dance in celebration of the coming new year: the Year of the Monkey. Directly opposite, competing for the attention of the crowd, and succeeding in drawing some of the younger spectators away from the dancers, a familiar global clown is performing tricks and handing out leaflets that announce McDonald's new 'Samurai Burgers'. The shop in front of me, saturated with all varieties of electronic goods, is attracting customers with the slogan 'the latest in modern technology'; the one behind, selling colourful fabrics and garments, is appealing to 'good old fashion values'.

My attention is momentarily caught by a woman in a green *batik* traditional dress, her head covered with a white purpose-made scarf, leaning backwards over the rails in a relaxed posture (does it belie her inner tension?), watching the world pass her by: elegantly attired Chinese women (flat chests, padded shoulders), smartly dressed Chinese men (coiffured hair, strong aftershaves) rushing to their next appointment, Indian couples (women in colourful 'Punjabi' dress), other women with their head covered accompanied (always?) by short, bearded men (some with turbans on their heads), and groups of

European and American men and women (most casually dressed) sniffing, admiring, picking display items from tables and shelves and then putting them back. The woman in the green *baju* appears passive, reflective. But the atmosphere is noisy. Somewhere in this Japanese shopping complex – 'Lot 10' – a disc jockey, who speaks with the accent and lingo of Afro-Americans, is playing a rap song that reverberates through the entire building: 'Pump up the Jam'. The rap music coming from everywhere fuses with the Chinese melody coming from below, and the two bounce off countless echoes from an array of shops playing their own brands of 'musak', merge with sound waves issuing from products on demonstration and drown the universal echo of continuous chatter.

I am in Kuala Lumpur, Malaysia. But I could, almost, be anywhere on the planet.

The plurality that one experiences in Kuala Lumpur, or indeed one can experience in any market place where all manner of world commodities are assembled under one roof and juxtaposed with all manner of ethnic cultures for the consumer to experience different worlds, is the plurality of postmodernism. Its familiar features that any one can experience in any big city, are the collapse of the old and the new, the values and virtues of instantaneity, the amalgamation of fact and fantasy and the consequent indistinction of the real and the imaginary, and the total absence of meaning and depth. Postmodernism is the dominant wave of the future: it is the arena of the cultural battles to come, the theatre where issues of meaning and purpose will be acted out, and the stage where non-Western people will define the 'I' of their Identity.

The end of the twentieth century brings mankind to the closing chapters of modernity – the European imperial adventure that began with Columbus and has its roots in the seventeenth century philosophical movement dubbed 'the Enlightenment'. The cultural order of modernity that emerged as the consequence of the discoveries of the 'new world' and instrumental reason was monolithic and oppressive. It posited Western civilization as the norm, the sole repository of Truth, the yardstick by which all 'Others' are to be measured. It saw history as a linear progress towards Western capitalism and liberal secularism, concluding with the transformation of the world into a single, global, Western civilisation. Capitalist economics, utilitarian industrialism, rationalised organisation, and the embracement of the new for the sake of the new was its credo. By definition, it considered what was not modern to be inferior and therefore unworthy of respect, dignity or survival.

The last fifty years have seen modernity play havoc with traditional cultures. In the name of 'development', old cities and communities have been diffused, displaced, destroyed. For the sake of 'progress', traditional ways of knowing – science, medicine, technologies – subjugated, suppressed, solidified in cement. To be 'modern', traditional lifestyles and cultures, disturbed, disrupted, dissolved into oblivion. The juggernaut of modernity has been running 'amok' – ironically, the only Malay word in the English language – speeding out-of-control towards a not-so-distant pile-up on the highway of history.

Today, the malaise associated with the experience of modernity is widely felt and openly acknowledged. Recent developments in such diverse fields of human inquiry as philosophy, sociology of knowledge, linguistics, literary theory, architecture, and literature have knocked the stuffing out of modernity, revealing it to be a rather pretentious turkey. Modernity is coming under attack from postmodernism. The champions of modernity wish to preserve its innate superiority (based on the notion that reason is the only criteria of truth) and desire to preserve it from being torn asunder by doubt and uncertainty. Postmodernist thought undermines all grand systems of thought that claim to be the sole arbiters of truth: reason is placed at par with magic, and all truth is considered relative in this best of all possible universes. Doubt is all. Relativity is the norm.

Whereas modernity oppressed and marginalised all non-western cultures, postmodernism opens the door for their re-entry into humanity and rejoices in the diversity and plurality of ethnic cultures. Whereas modernity placed Western Values, Western History, Western Cultures, Western Visions at the apex of human experience and endeavour, postmodernism levels all values, all histories, all cultures, all visions onto a uniform plane, emphasising and celebrating their differences. Whereas modernity suppressed non-Western voices, postmodernity seeks to represent other cultures and give their voices an opportunity to be heard.

But postmodernism is not the first chapter (the 'Introduction' as it were) of a new book of our destiny. It marks the realisation that many rationally constructed predictions of the nineteenth century have turned out to be more wrong than the irrational illusions they were supposed to replace. Postmodernism represents a partial displacement from repression to seduction, from the police to the market, from the army to the bank, from the depth reading of epistemology to a surface reading of hermeneutics. It is the no-man's land where the concluding chapters of modernity disintegrate into meaninglessness, and the outlines of a new book, that will eventually take its place, are being worked out. Postmodernism is the desert where people are prospecting for a new form of existence, as the remaining vestiges of modernity crumble to dust all around them. This prospecting, the shaping of a future book of our modes of social and cultural existence, will necessarily lead to considerable strife and conflict. But beyond this conflict, one can envision and work for the emergence of a saner, safer, society.

When the pendulum swings it swings from one extreme to another. Both modernity and postmodernity are extremities: one the flip side of the other. The next fifty years will be dominated with conflicts that result from such violent swings: from modernism to postmodernism, from a totally closed society to a completely open (and exposed) one, from liberal anarchy to fundamentalist rigidity. These swings represent our attempts to define ourselves, to heal our selfhoods after the devastation of modernity. We learn only through experience; and it is only by working out all extreme positions of our cultural identity from our system that we will come to realise what traditional thought had always taught us: that our salvation as different cultures and societies lies in following 'the middle path', the path of balance and accommodation – a path that is reached when the pendulum comes to rest.

When the pendulum finally comes to rest – around fifty years hence – we will have discovered that the world cannot be ruled either by a single notion of truth, nor can it be dominated by an ideology where all truths are relative and, ultimately, none really matter. We will have realised that our quest for total freedom from tradition (modernity), or our total indifferent dissolution in a collection of cultures, suspends us in a darkness where all things are regarded with equal disbelief and indifference. We will then be in the first chapter of the book of genuine multiculturalism. We will be in a multicivilizational and multicultural world. It will not be a world of 'civilization as we know it': both modernism and postmodernism are ultimately about maintaining a world in the single image of Western civilization. It will be a world of civilizations – Western, Islamic, Indian, Chinese, and numerous smaller ones. Each civlization will rediscover and renovate itself according to its own criteria and concepts and have its own dynamic, thriving ways of knowing, doing and being. Each will discover its own forms of participatory governance, democratic autonomy and civilizational identity. And all will enrich each other with mutual respect, cooperation and synthesis: a world of different civilizations *ipso facto* recognises both the interdependent and relational nature of identities, their elements of incommensurability and their political right of autonomy. In such a world, one can easily acknowledge and appreciate the truths and values of other civilizations, without legitimately renouncing a serious interest in one's own.

Identity is about belonging. A multicivilizational world furnishes one not just with a national or ethnic identity: it places one in the parameters of a civilization with all that a civilization entails and thus simultaneously provides one with a more solid foundation for one's identity as well as liberating one's Selfhood from parochial concerns. One is thus in a position both to respect the concerns of others as well as pursue one's own concerns within one's civilization. Each individual is the synthesis not only of existing relations but of the history of these relations. She/he is a precis of the past and the present. We must thus seek our own individual identities within the context of our own history, tradition, culture and civilization. We have to articulate, in the intersection of our everyday lives, the economic, political and gender relations of subordination and domination that exist within our own cultures and civilizations. The individual then has a great deal of work to do, both to define the 'I' of the Identity and to slow down, indeed stop, the violent swing of the pendulum from one extreme to another. The alternative to a multicivilizational world which establishes our sense of selfhood has already been worked out by Nietzsche: madness. Beyond the conflicts that lie ahead in eastern Europe, the Muslim world, the North–South divide and traditional/modern dichotomy, is a new book of visions waiting to be written. But it will be a hard book to write, involving each individual and continuous effort. Above all, it requires an appreciation and understanding of Other cultures that goes far beyond simple tolerance based on lack of interest or disbelief. Indifference is the prescription for madness. The first step we can take as individuals towards writing the initial chapters of the new book is to take ourselves and our beliefs and all Others and their beliefs more seriously.

As I sip my cappucino, and plot my next move to increase the resistance that will eventually bring the pendulum to rest and usher me towards a more balanced existence, I reflect on the numerous ways my identity is compromised, confiscated and condemned. The global capitalism of which this shopping mall is a concrete manifestation, does not really care whether I am Muslim, Christian, secularist, Pakistani, male, black or whatever: it simply demands that I buy. Here, in this cultural desert, in this plurality of indifference, both my being and my identity are a function of the very act of buying. I shop, therefore I am. My identity is shaped by the image that I purchase: designer clothes, the right car, the right briefcase, the appropriate watch – I am buying a sign system, the brand gives me my identity, that's why brand names are worth killing for.

I become conscious of approving glances. I am wearing Levi jeans (supported by a Dunhill belt), a YSL T-shirt, Nike sneakers, and a Rolex watch that I constantly fiddle with and adjust on my left wrist. A large group of Japanese tourists size me up, nod appreciatingly and walk by. I feel like a million dollars. Only the women in traditional green *baju*, still leaning on the rails, disapproves: traitor.

Everything I am wearing is fake: made in Thailand, and none the worse for it. I hope inside, somewhere deep inside, within the body that imprisons my soul, there is a real me. I walk out of 'Dèlifrance' to search for my Self.

A FUTURE
FROM WITHIN

John Dakin

'. . . the Chinese philosopher contemplating the Iron horse of the Celestial Railway, neatly punctures the absoluteness of . . . rationalistic materialistic certitude. . . . The engineer says "Isn't it marvellous? We just put water and fire into it and look! it goes along, and it pulls all these carriages" "Yes" answers the philosopher "You designed it to do exactly those things. So it does them."'.

It is a reasonable view that if humanity continues to behave as at present, the life-support provided by the global ecological system risks being impaired beyond its capacity to sustain us.

It is an entirely new fact of our situation that we are now all in it together. We have moved from being global simply as a species to the necessity of being global also as a society. We are challenged to expand our sociality out beyond the boundaries of the present nation-state. Our 170 or so existing societies must learn to be members of a society of the world – law-abiding, tolerant, and accommodating – good global citizens.

Over millennia, we have learned to live in ever larger and more sophisticated social groupings. It is therefore legitimate to envision that inherently we possess the capacity to reach the level of society required for ensuring our ecological safety.

But against this optimistic view we have to array those obscure and doubtful elements in our situation which weight the scales against us. Countless other species have already died out. The earth's natural order offers no opinion about our survival being predestined.

My chapter tries to probe one of these obscure elements: the appropriateness or otherwise of our contemporary Western mindset, and the way it is changing. Its present form suggests it could help or hinder our survival.

Since about mid-century, when Bertrand de Jouvenel began to develop a scientific approach to futures – his *The Art of Conjecture*, coming out of *Futuribles*, was the seminal book – 'serious' prediction of the future has been mostly along conscious-rational lines, using logic-based methods such as computer modelling. We feel secure in the supposed safety of our conscious rationality, the here and now of our day-to-day 'reality', which supports this approach.

But how secure is it? The evidence of psychology, anthropology, and the study of religion and art demonstrate that humans do not behave solely on what scientific rationalism may offer. As well as consciousness, we possess – or are possessed by – an unconscious mental process – individual and collective – having its own hidden agenda.

We make a mistake in generally assuming our rationality is fixed, when in fact it is more like a boat journeying down a river. The boat does have its own power, but the stream also moves it along. The helmsman does have some choice, but is without a reliable chart of the river. It may be hastening towards a waterfall, or about to meander aimlessly, split into the many channels of a delta, or the fury of turbulent rapids.

What is this stream that carries us along, and from time to time wrecks our fragile boat of rational discourse? It is all the aspects and dimensions of our conscious and unconscious *experience* of living. We mistake the boat for the total reality, and therefore do not pay attention to the fact that the fragile boat of our conscious rationality is carried along by something much more powerful than its own engines.

Predictions warn us of a waterfall ahead. We hope to avoid it by looking for navigable rapids, perhaps flowing parallel with it. The waterfall is the global ecological disaster we shall suffer if we continue on our present course of highly exploitative industrialism. Navigating the rapids successfully calls for taking appropriate thought and action in time.

We may think what we generate in the boat determines whether we go over the waterfall, or find a channel round it, or get lost in endless meanderings. But if we look at the stream, we see it too is carrying predictions, possibilities, threats, and potential future events.

We do not know whether we ought to think the boat, or the river, is in charge of the situation. If we think the river is, then we are fatalists, and as good as drowned. If we think the boat is *wholly* in charge, our egotism will probably lead to the same result.

The sections that follow will look more closely at what is going on in the boat. It is hopeful that science and technology could correct many mistakes and avert some dangers. Using them, we could successfully address many material aspects of the future. But especially now we need to look at the river, probing for any intentions it may have for the boat, and those in it. Not hopeful are our lack of global sociality, our proclivity for war, and our failure to control science, technology, and production-distribution for globally social ends.

From the eighteenth century Enlightenment onwards, our conscious, rational mental process has been hugely and exponentially successful in handling the material world to our human advantage – although not equitably.

The story of the Chinese philosopher contemplating the iron horse of the Celestial Railway, neatly punctures the absoluteness of this rationalistic-materialistic certitude. He and the engineer (a Westerner) are admiring the newly-arrived locomotive. The engineer says:

'Isn't it marvellous? We just put water and fire into it, and look! it goes along, and pulls all these carriages.'

'Yes,' answers the philosopher 'You designed it to do exactly those things. So it does them.'

We forget our science and technology come only from ourselves. They work if we do our investigation and design properly. But if we do not, they can produce nonsense, like the phlogiston theory of fire, or the flying machine that flapped its wings.

With this kind of truth we can make many predictions with a high likelihood of fulfilment, such as a sustainable technology of energy production based on the photovaltaic process, that the increased use of fibre optics will accelerate the spread of all the electronic technologies generally, or the applications of nanotechnology. But we cannot predict how humans will use this knowledge, or how they will react to it in feeling.

The notion that the truth of science-technology is the 'real' truth relies on nothing more than our believing that it is so. Attaching value to science and technology thus ultimately rests on the demonstrable fact that humans have beliefs. But the truth of the *content* of a belief is not scientifically provable.

The contents of beliefs change. They come and go according to the various pressures on them. When a belief is questioned, its power begins to decline, and it is eventually dumped. If, however, it has psychological truth on its side, it may return.

Resuming our metaphor, the belief that supports science, technology, and business lives in the waters of the river. The boat is supported by the river, watertight as long as it is sound. But what is in the water can also rot its timbers, and cause it to founder.

Such rotting is already well advanced for our present Western boat of narrow technological rationality. Many of the planks are unsound, although the boat still floats, and still carries some of us along. Others, however, have been progressively abandoning this boat for about a hundred and fifty years, because of the gradual erosion of its sustaining belief. But societies at large still cling to the positivistic and materialistic view of life it generates and nourishes.

This materialistic emphasis can be easily demonstrated by asking: What is our contemporary bottom line?

We still profess the primacy of religion – Western Christianity, despite multiculturalism – and theoretically we value the arts highly. But of course we do not seriously *live* by these activities, or their values. Privately, we feel we survive primarily through economic effort. That is the operational real first value. Most real for us are the material goods of physical existence, and getting the wherewithal for continued enjoyment of them. Next valued are the political means for capturing the economic benefits.

We have had wonderful aspirations, and some achievement, of material well-being for all. The social-philanthropic movement of the last century, democratic socialist and communist-socialist statism, new town, universal pensions, doctoring, and education have been some of the means. Winning these has been fuelled by forces ranging from genteel benevolence to militant revolutionary millennialism.

This materialism has been accompanied by its own idealism. We really were convinced that by taking conscious thought we could make better societies, protecting people against the more outrageous misfortunes. Forget about blessedness in the hereafter; let's have it here and now. The sentiments were seductive, but they were not psychologically or culturally very solidly backed.

Strangely, it is this alliance of rationalism and materialism-idealism that has brought us to the present concern about the safety of the biosphere. Science provides the information about the harm we are doing to the earth's ecological system, and suggests remedies. Materialistic idealism injects a guilty feeling that we have gone too far, and must change our behaviour.

The materialist and idealistic planks of the boat are therefore now as much under attack as those of our conscious rationalism. For the same reasons: their supporting belief has been eroding for some time, and at an accelerating pace.

Suffering is the main concomitant of this erosion. Suffering due to economic hardship, social disintegration, violence, and loss of the sense of stability and security is a manifest cause of loss of confidence in materialistic values. We learn very quickly when we suffer.

But it is important to note here that the crucial suffering is predicted – something to come in the future, unless . . . Now, therefore, we are in possession of the knowledge *before* the suffering actually hits. This is the obverse of the familiar process of learning through actually experiencing the suffering, and is an entirely new psychological situation.

Can we learn to act *prospectively* before the catastrophe and the suffering become accomplished fact? Can we transform consciousness to achieve this end?

The crucial suffering to be avoided can come along several routes. Present societies may collapse under their own weight, perhaps because of trying to move in contradictory directions, say, toward sustainability, and simultaneously toward aggressive economic growth, or they may fail to generate a world society. Or, they may trigger something in the biosphere that will set off major climatic changes that drastically upset societies, through failing water and food supplies, and collapsed economies.

If we continue as we are, either one, or more, of these possibilities may be on the cards. Any one would produce massive, widespread serious suffering which we could be too late to forestall completely. But if we are lucky, and take thought, we may suffer enough initially to make us change our ways before our ability to recoup slips irretrievably from our grasp.

Two accelerators of the decline of present social structures are: changes in production processes that reduce the amount of labour required, and the drive of nation-states to cluster together in great trading blocs. There are also subsidiary causes, such as large national debts, governments living beyond their means, and social rigidities and obsolescent values that inhibit rapid, intelligent response. Over all, looms the corporate global control of production and distribution through giant autonomous conglomerate companies, impersonal, faceless, footloose across the world, and owing allegiance to no particular nation-state.

Suffering will be experienced not only through the individual losing employment, or having to settle for a poorer job, but simultaneously the services built up by the social democratic societies, will be increasingly unsustainable. Some of them will first be reduced; some will be eliminated.

The general trend now – first stage of the suffering – is to thrust as much as possible back on to the individual. Governments and employers steadily divest themselves of responsibility for the citizen and the worker. He or she pays more for unemployment and health insurance, pays ever higher taxes, and feels under ever heavier pressure through more hours being worked, and higher skills and ever greater productivity being demanded. Unfortunately, the natural endowment of individuals does not increase correspondingly.

In Canada, for example, the elimination of one of the two old age pensions has already begun, and senior governments are systematically reducing transfer payments for social and other services to lower levels of government which in turn must increase local taxes, as present forms of society and standards of living become unsustainable.

Under these emerging circumstances, all sorts of physical and institutional arrangements become no longer workable. Single family houses are found to be too big and possibly too numerous. Commercial real estate is overcapitalized because of reduced spending by the public – *in*conspicuous consumption. Much factory space becomes wrongly located, in the wrong country for the only labour market the company can now afford. Production loses touch with real needs since only profit determines what shall be produced. To cap it all, there is the growing seepage of cheap labour and alien cultural patterns into the developed countries, with assorted demographic 'time bombs'.

These changes are already spawning harsher attitudes toward minorities, unemployed and displaced persons, and toward employees generally. The springs of human kindness dry up. Such trends, if not restrained, can lead to the non-society – de-socialized human beings, predators on each other, savagely fighting one another for survival.

However, concern for the social whole is not dead. Its values are not utterly abandoned; they may yet fulfil Arthur Schlesinger Jnr's prediction that governments will swing back to social concern during the nineties. The humane concern for the social good is not, of course, confined to the political left, but in a polarised world, it tends to gather there, rather than on the right. The battle for how the benefits of production are to be distributed continues, both inside the nation-state and globally.

All this hits us just at the moment when humanity as a whole must collaborate in taking serious thought for restructuring societies so that the damage they are causing to the biosphere can be checked.

We are thus facing two areas of crisis for societies: that of our societies being highly stressed within themselves and in relating to each other globally, and that of human society as a whole being challenged to ensure the continuance of its life-support in the natural world.

Considering our entanglement in narrowly rationalistic and materialistic values, and our having allowed these to form societies of the kind we now have, the problem essentially boils down to discovering how best to think and feel about our situation.

It is helpful to begin with cultural and psychological matters because these are 'upstream' of all other areas of mental activity. Here, we can go straight for the jugular, and ask: What happens on these planes of experience when we sense the deterioration of our existing values and social systems? How do we typically react to such realization?

Resuming the boat metaphor, our common response is to jump overboard, committing ourselves directly to the river itself. In psychological terms, this means we abandon the now disintegrating boat of our old rationality, and return to the immediate experience of living as the most reliable mental base on which to function. Old values, dogmas, rules, and explanations suddenly become irrelevant. The individual comes to feel the new experience to be a psychological support self-evidently superior to the old rationality.

The signs of this principle have been all about us during this century. They are strongly manifest in the arts. The key painters, for example, began by nearly completely severing connection with the world we see (cubism, etc.) and retreating into worlds of their own construction. Only gradually have they returned to the outer world, to restructure it from new interior positions.

Because they have not yet acutely felt the collapse of inherited systems of thought, feeling, action, and society, most people have been baffled by such painters as Braque, Picasso, and Klee. They have not felt much compulsion to return to direct experience, but have been satisfied with hearsay reports of it. But this compulsion will come in our future experience, perhaps is already present in rock and other music, in which total immersion is the whole point. The painters, and other artists, have simply been ahead of the rest of us in sensing the disintegration of systems, and therefore have already faced the question: When the old psychological, cultural, and social syntheses dissolve, how are we to look out upon the world?

Similarly religion. Evangelical, and other religions emphasizing direct spiritual experience, have flourished, while more formal, 'social' religions have suffered decline. Western enthusiasm for Eastern religions and philosophies that seek the direct experience of existence, Zen Buddhism's 'satori', is another manifestation of the phenomenon.

Mass sport and fanatical party or group allegiance to a cause are also evidence. In these, as in fascism, nazism, communism, and even in our domestic issues like civil rights or abortion, the individual seeks, and may achieve fresh, direct experience.

As the suffering increases, we shall pursue this direct experience ever more avidly. Our psychological condition will exact this price, as it did in the disintegration of the Graeco-Roman civilization. The new, direct experience which people craved then was provided especially by the many mystery religions. Eastern and indigenous purveyors of sometimes dubious salvation who now batten on the fears and sufferings of Western and other publics are an obvious parallel.

The *desire* for the direct experience, then, is already a genuine, hard psychological fact of contemporary life in the developed countries and elsewhere. This may be counted an optimistic sign since new psychic energy will be released, despite the danger that it can also lead to destructive fanaticism. Without a new flow of psychic energy we cannot possibly make the next great jump – to the society of the world, either rebuilding our present boat of rationality, or constructing an entirely new one.

The transition from the Graeco-Roman cultural and psychological set to the new outlook of the Western Middle Ages took a long time. But gradually a new rationality boat was constructed, and a highly refined level of rational consciousness, culminating in Thomas Aquinas, was achieved. By his time, however, that boat's planks were already rotting. Toward the end of his life, in the face of new direct experience, Thomas himself declared his rationally constructed writings to be but straw.

The general hypothesis is that we swing through a cycle whose dynamics begin in direct experience of predominantly either the external or the internal world. From this, rational systems (boats) are gradually constructed, providing rules for running societies and guiding individual mental life. Finally, through suffering, as the system fails in effectiveness for survival, we have to search again for the direct experience on which to build rationally anew.

Where are we now in this cycle? As mass societies, we are not yet utterly convinced the old systems have deteriorated beyond retrieval. We talk about 'sustainable development'. This may be quite possible; many archaic societies have achieved it. But the present Western connotation of the phrase is that we can sustain the global ecological system in an adequate state for continuing to support us, while yet simultaneously pressing on with our aggressive, exploitative economic growth through societies as at present structured. Such 'eco-capitalism' hopes to eat its cake and have it.

Very possibly there is a period in front of us during which social, cultural, and psychological disintegration will have to be suffered until a critical mass of a country's population comes to a full recognition that the old system no longer works. At that point, the construction of the new arrangements – psychological, cultural, and social – will already be under way through the contributions of the forerunning direct experiencers.

Meantime, how ironic that Third World populations scramble to take up what the developed countries are coming to see they have to abandon! They struggle to lift themselves out of the water, and on to our disintegrating boat – quite literally at times – unaware of the dangers it faces.

In comparison with the Graeco-Roman civilization, the modern world as a whole has the great advantage of an enormous body of scientific knowledge, stored in centres distributed worldwide. This is unlikely to be lost through the collapse of any one society, or even of a group of societies. The Graeco-Roman world did not pass on its science very well, although something survived.

Although our boat is better built and larger than theirs, it is still subject to attack by whatever is in the river. Therefore, there may come a time when support for science (our essential rationality) fades in the West. This may seem unlikely at the moment, but failing interest in science in schools and increasing reliance by the general public on luck, what the stars foretell, misunderstandings about what science is, and a general flight from reason are ominous signs.

Yet, supposing we escape the waterfall, science and technology must survive the rapids – on the old boat reconstructed, or on a new boat. The reason for insisting on this is that purely quantitatively we cannot maintain our now huge human population by any other means. The key question is whether we can learn to put these splendid assets wholeheartedly to human use.

Finally, what can be said to assist positive thinking into the future? Perhaps most important is to formulate the problem as clearly as possible. Here, there is plenty of room for differences of approach. For me, the logic of the material presented here leads to the following problem:

How do we reach an adequate level of cooperation as a species to ensure survival, in the context of having to maintain the life support capability of the earth in productivity and stability, even while yet strongly pursuing economic development?

If this states the core of our dilemma, then it follows there must be appropriate conscious action on our part, and that this will be achievable only through the fact that human beings function best in societies. This means the idea of society is the key. It is for this reason social ecologists concentrate their attention on the relation of society to the biosphere. Murray Bookchin urges we must aim for:

'. . . the reharmonization of humanity with nature through the reharmonization of human with human, the achievement of an ecological society structured on ecologically sound technologies and face-to-face democratic communities.' (Bookchin, 1990)

But to function globally, society has to be global, with global government, laws, enforcement, and – most important – the willing assent of all members. These would be the present nation-states, plus certain 'estates', such as scientific, corporate, and other bodies. We do not yet have any such global government, but there are some beginnings, such as the peacekeeping function of the UN, the development of international law, trade agreements, and the globalization of science, technology, and business.

How are the nation-state societies to achieve a society of the world? The time-honoured technique for fusing together existing societies has ranged from an agreed coalescence, to single conquest through the imperial ambition of one state with the power to coerce others.

An example of the coalescence route is the forging of the European Community, now joined by the European Free Trade Area countries, and perhaps later by some eastern Europeans and parts of the old USSR. These activities can be counted increasingly valuable experience for moving us toward the saving of the species.

The other extreme would be empire by a single power. This does not now seem feasible. The next best thing for those with such ambition would be the vigorous promotion of a particular set of values, attitudes, and institutions, leading to the domination of a particular lifestyle. This may be possible. The obvious aspirant is the USA, which seems genuinely to believe its values have a universal rightness which all must surely acknowledge. The cold fact, of course, is quite different.

Observing this, a serious difficulty obstructing global cooperation emerges. Eastern and Western conventional beliefs about human and other life, and their relation to the rest of existence, are vastly different. Carl Jung commented that the West has an '. . . evolutionary cosmogony with a beginning and end' and cannot accept the ' . . . idea of a static, self-contained, eternal cycle of events' which is the core of Eastern belief. The Westerner insists on finding meaning in it all and has ' . . . shifted all emphasis to the here and now.' This is alien to Eastern belief and feeling.

The cohesive principle of a society of the world will have to negotiate this difference. Only an over-arching conviction of the urgent need to act survival-effectively might do this. But what will generate that conviction strongly enough to overcome our drive for separateness and short-term partisan gain by nation-states?

No doubt widespread global suffering could force us into a global society capable of creating the institutions for keeping our behaviour within the rules of the earth's ecological system. But this brings us back to the situation that we can only get the necessary result if we act before the suffering seriously develops. Operationally, this is what we now have to do first.

The deepest psychological part of our problem may well be to discover just how to do that. The spirit of the coming time will therefore need to be the quest for the direct experience.

Our knowledge and experience are grounds for hope that we can reinforce our present boat, or build a new one, and circumvent the waterfall. The earth has enough landscape for ten billion of us, and we could produce and distribute enough protein to feed that number. We can be optimistic in this perspective.

But the question is whether the river is going to yield a new consciousness of ourselves as a global totality in the social perspective, and, supposing that vision is forthcoming from the depths of our psyches, whether we shall find the self-knowledge, will, and moral stature to take the necessary action. Optimism along this perspective is not so easily justified.

NOTES

Conscious-rational. We hate to admit we are influenced to think, feel, and act by non-conscious processes. But the evidence of psychology shows our unconscious has a very big say. If this understanding is applied to futures thinking, we have to suspect we may be moving in directions we consciously know nothing about. We now recognize the European Enlightenment was not the universal dawn after the long night of 'superstition' it presented itself to be.

Waterfall ahead. No one, in writing or TV presentations, has put the case for staving off ecological disaster better than David Suzuki.

Abandoning the rationalistic boat. From Schopenhauer onwards, at least. Kierkegaard, Nietzsche, the existentialists, etc. – all men of the direct experience, behind them Rousseau and the Romantics.

Graeco-Roman world. See Hans Jonas. *The Gnostic Religion: The Message of the Alien God and the beginnings of Christianity.* Beacon Press, Boston 1958.

Aquinas and mystic Meister Eckhart were near contemporaries, the latter a man of the direct experience par excellence – required when the medieval synthesis collapsed.

Memories, Dreams, Reflections by C.G. Jung. Anita Jaffe ed. Vintage Books, New York 1989, 316. Jung's work becomes increasingly relevant to our entire human situation. Likewise, psychologist Abraham Maslow stresses the return to the direct experience. But on the East–West difference it is possible there is no dilemma at the deepest psychological level. See Hubert Benoit. *The Supreme Doctrine: Psychological Studies in Zen Thought.* Viking, New York 1959, xiv.

Man-Nature. The differences between Eastern and Western views come out clearly in comparing primate studies. Linda M. Fedigan and P.J. Asquith. *The Monkeys of Azashiyama: Thirty-five Years of Research in Japan and the West.* State University of New York Press, Albany 1991.

THE PROMISE OF THE 21ST CENTURY

Richard Slaughter

'. . . when a right relationship is re-established between people, culture and technology a whole new world of options emerges.'

The end of one millennium and the prospect of another to follow is not merely symbolic; it provides us with an opportunity to take stock and consider our position. Why are such turning points important? They reflect two powerful aspects of our reality. One is the capacity (even the need) of the human mind to range at will over time past, present and future. The other is the fact of our interconnectedness with all things past and future.

During the course of everyday life we become entrained in short-term, ego-bound, thinking, in the limited demands of the present. But the transition into a new century reminds us of the wider process which willy-nilly we participate in. Looking back over the last hundred years we contemplate our roots in the lives and cultures of our parents and their parents. Over the next hundred years we look forward with our children and theirs to the world which is growing organically, day by day, from our present reality. This 'two-hundred year present' is our space in time. And when we reach the changeover, as dictated by the calendar and our numbering system, for a brief moment we seem to stand on a pivot of history.

The perspective catches our imagination. It is, perhaps, the temporal equivalent of the view from a high mountain. The details which had absorbed us stand revealed in a breathtaking panorama. Yet that is where the analogy ends. For we are keenly aware that the 20th century has been harrowing for us, for the Earth and certainly for our children. It is highly significant that at the end of the 19th century people looked ahead with optimism and hope. They believed that the rational application of scientific knowledge and technical skill would re-make the world and usher in an era of peace and prosperity. Nowadays it takes a profound act of imagination to re-construct that sense of boundless possibility. For we carry the experience of the souring of that dream, of wars, catastrophes and the steady deterioration of our prospects and our images of the future.

Approaching the new millennium we know at a deep, incontrovertible level that everything is at stake. As Macy puts it:

> With isolated exceptions, every generation prior to ours has lived with the assumption that other generations would follow . . . Now we have lost the certainty that we will have a future. I believe this loss, felt at some level of consciousness by everyone, regardless of political orientation, is the pivotal psychological reality of our time. (Macy 1991)

There is no transcendent principle which says that the experiment of life on planet Earth must succeed. Our very success as a species, coupled with the extraordinary assumptions and habits of the industrial era have brought us to a real 'hinge in history', not an imaginary one or merely a calendar change. So it is not surprising that people have come to fear the future. Someone once called it 'a disaster that had already happened!' To the extent that substances such as plutonium will be around for up to 250,000 years, or that the viability of forests and other ecosystems is threatened, that could be true. However, it is also possible that a keen awareness of both halves of this two-hundred year period may, in fact, stimulate changes, shifts of perception, processes and actions which could lead in an entirely different direction.

There is, of course, a danger here of wishful thinking, of 'finding good in everything', a silver lining in every cloud. That is not what I am suggesting. We are in very great peril – a fact which is already fully appreciated by the collective unconscious (otherwise, why would images of disaster, decay and decline dominate our popular and visual media?). But, properly handled, that fact may jolt us into a new awareness of where we are and what we need to do. It is most emphatically not a case of thinking good thoughts and being good, positive people. We may need to get angry. The point is that we face a challenge of unprecedented proportions. We have known it for some time. But late industrial culture has provided us with so many diversions and avoidance strategies that most of us are simply not paying attention.

The approach of a new century provides a genuine chance to take stock. We must look back at the horrors of the century: at Auschwitz, Hiroshima, Bhopal and the rest. We must be able to look right into the abyss – and then beyond it to the processes of recovery and renewal which point in quite different directions. This is not an illusion. There is plenty of evidence that within the vast span of human cultures and responses there can be found all the resources necessary to re-conceptualise our predicament and steer in a different direction. It is from this viewpoint that we can discuss, indeed more than discuss, create, the promise of the 21st century, for promise there is.

One of the most encouraging things I have observed from meeting people, monitoring the literature and reflecting on the implications is *the emergence of a deep consensus* about our predicament and what is needed to change it. It seems to me that there is a genuine congruence of insight emerging from many places and many cultures. There is no conspiracy, no blueprint. But there is an emerging view of reality which could help us to construct truly post-industrial cultures. So, while social learning is slow, while there are enormous lags in virtually all our important systems (government, business, education, economics etc.), it is possible to discern a way out of the trap we have constructed:

* Recover a sense of the future
* Create institutions and processes of foresight
* Repair the damage, reduce risk
* Create sustainable economies
* Release the potential within people
* Find new purposes and meanings
* Re-discover intrinsic value
* Re-invent culture via a renewed worldview

RECOVERING A SENSE OF THE FUTURE

Many cultures, including Western ones, have and have had a clearly-articulated relationship to the future. Native Americans, for example, were known to consider the seventh generation in their decision-making councils. Yet the cultural editing of most contemporary Western cultures has had two contradictory effects. In some ways it has mis-represented the future dimension as a kind of empty space, an abstraction, which is not worthy of serious attention. That is one reason why school curricula embody so many references to the past, but so few to the future. On the other hand two very different types of future images have become current in late-industrial cultures. One is the optimistic, high-tech, machine-dominated version which is found on popular TV and in young people's books. The other is the dark vision of dystopia, of decline, decay and eventual destruction.

Now while it may be true that both represent real alternatives, with roots in aspects of the present, neither begin to do justice to the much wider range of options and possibilities that lie ahead. Activating a developed sense of the latter is very important for four good reasons: decisions have long-term consequences; future alternatives imply present choices; forward thinking is preferable to crisis management; further transformations are certain to occur.

DECISIONS HAVE LONG–TERM CONSEQUENCES

Every decision is a branch-point. It leads away from one end and toward another. This is how the world is shaped. While some decisions are trivial and become lost in the texture of larger events, others powerfully condition the present and future. The survival or extinction of entire species is now dependent upon human decisions about their habitats. Decisions to deploy certain chemicals, technologies, weapons systems all affect the viability of our environment and our prospects for a livable future. If we continue to pour resources into negative and damaging enterprises, the odds will continue to mount up against us. If we could alter the cultural programming we might see things differently. We might pursue qualitative growth and pour our ingenuity into restoring the earth and healing the damage.

FUTURE ALTERNATIVES IMPLY PRESENT CHOICES

The power of the human mind to range at will across the vast span of past, present and future provides us with a powerful means of controlling which ends we pursue. We are not (yet) locked into a mechanical process which dictates our future. Since we can envisage many different possibilities, we have freedom of choice.

To the extent that we become aware of different future alternatives, we gain access to new choices in the present. If we become aware of something we want to avoid we can take appropriate action. Similarly, if we can imagine something we want to create, we can set in motion the means to create it. This is as true of a relationship as it is of a new car model or airport.

Future alternatives imply present choices because it takes time to exert our will and mobilise the resources involved in doing something or avoiding it.

FORWARD THINKING IS PREFERABLE TO CRISIS MANAGEMENT

It follows that foresight has now become a structural necessity for societies in transition, rather than merely a matter of personal prudence and safety. Forward thinking is preferable to crisis management because the latter is expensive and wasteful. Furthermore, as the Chernobyl example tragically proved, the ensuing damage may be more costly than anyone would rationally contemplate. While it is not possible to predict the future states of social systems in any detail, it is possible to take a strategic view, to explore options and alternatives, and to anticipate eventualities.

Forward thinking creates a decision context in which unpleasant surprises can be minimised. It means that crises can be kept to a minimum. As the stakes mount, so it becomes increasingly important to invest in foresight (Slaughter, 1990).

FURTHER TRANSFORMATIONS ARE CERTAIN TO OCCUR

One thing which we can know for certain is that if the present dynamism of our social and technical systems continues, we will continue to be faced with radical changes in every aspect of our lives. The changes in prospect over the next 100 years are probably as great, or greater than those which have occurred over the last 1,000. They may well include: the loss of most remaining tropical forests; major climate shifts; new person/machine interactions; significant life-extension; increasingly powerful computers, expert systems etc. and powerful new technologies (eg nanotechnology).

The fact of continuing rapid change in so many areas creates a major challenge for the species. Can we adapt? Should we adapt? How can these changes be regulated for the benefit of all? The futures dimension in general, and the study of futures in particular clearly has a role to play in posing, and attempting to answer such questions.

CREATING INSTITUTIONS AND PROCESSES OF FORESIGHT

In some ways we have known how important foresight is for a long time. That is why the following maxims have become validated through long traditional usage:

★ *look before you leap*
★ *a stitch in time saves nine*
★ *forewarned is forearmed.*

Such sayings establish the fundamental legitimacy of the foresight principle. Our species long ago learned that it is better to look ahead and to make provision for what may happen, than to let things take their course regardless. Successful foresight is clearly preferable to clearing up the mess. But how can foresight be 'successful' when social futures cannot be forecast or predicted?

Everyone applies the foresight principle in their daily lives. We check the weather before leaving home. We consider the options before taking a new course or beginning a new job. We make provision for contingencies by accumulating a financial 'nest egg' or taking out insurance. All this is common practice. Foresight raises no major problems at the individual level because it is part of the standard mental equipment of most normal people and its utility is unquestioned. But foresight at the social level is more problematic. It is not yet well supported because its utility has not been widely perceived and the institutional equivalents to our mental capacities have not yet been constructed and assembled. Why is this?

As noted above we have inherited a set of assumptions and presuppositions which condition our view of the world in various ways. Among many other things they tell us that the past is authoritative and real, that the short-term present is all that matters and that the future can be safely ignored. So this world view *actively discourages* any social investment in foresight even though, at a more personal level, we know it to be essential. Future-discounting can therefore be seen as one of the perceptual defects carried over from the scientific revolution and the industrial way of life.

This is not to say that organised foresight work does not exist. It does exist, but it is not normally available to the public. Every large organisation has discovered that it must plan. It must look ahead and develop strategic responses to its environment. Otherwise the product fails, the supply of essential parts runs out, the enemy's plans were better and the battle is lost. The sad story of Chernobyl graphically illustrates the costs to be expected when foresight is not correctly implemented and applied.

Techniques have been developed to facilitate systematic foresight in some limited contexts. However, the results of this work tend to be proprietory, fragmented and difficult to obtain. Given the fact of rapid structural change and growing environmental uncertainty, some means of abstracting the best available material, filling in the gaps and making the results publicly available are undoubtedly needed. Foresight work in the public interest has now become a structural necessity.

REPAIRING THE DAMAGE, REDUCING RISK

Given the enormous costs which the industrial system has exacted upon the world, repairing the damage has become a major imperative. There are very many areas and ecosystems which have been completely destroyed. Others have been severely compromised; entire species of plants and animals have been lost. This dynamic of destruction must be replaced with a new dynamic of restoration. Hence there is scope for a series of new professions to develop from the confluence of ecological science and environmental activism.

Beyond this there is a dawning possibility that humans may, in some sense, be able to 'reinvent nature.' Of course, this instantly recalls the notion of *hubris*, or unjustified pride. But in a different cultural context, one which had re-established a sense of the sacred and incorporated a strong stewardship ethic, it is conceivable that one part of nature (humans) could act *with* other parts (animals, plants, ecosystems) to create new patterns of life. If habitats can be recovered and restored there may be no reason why future humans should not reanimate extinct species (by reconstructing their DNA from numerous individual samples), adapt existing species (as is now being done with many crops and transgenic transfers) and invent new ones. *When guided by a higher ethic humans might actually improve upon what nature has achieved blindly.*

However, for any of this to happen, and to be viable, the present serious risk factors would need to be reduced or eliminated: stocks of nuclear weapons, military action, overpopulation, further deterioration of ecosystems and genetic pools. Resolving these is a *sine qua non* of a viable future (Tough 1991).

CREATING SUSTAINABLE ECONOMIES

This will not be easy, but in a sense it could be inevitable because a non-sustainable economy is just that. However, there are many contradictions to resolve. Advertising, consumerism, materialism, competitive individualism and the pursuit of old-style growth all make it difficult to embark on the transition.

Growth will need to be re-defined. Resources will need to be revalued and seen in their wider context. The environment will need to be brought fully into all economic calculations instead of being dismissed as a mere 'externality.' Energy will need to be conserved and used much more efficiently. At a deeper level, the ideologies and power systems which drive the technocratic machine will have to be challenged and replaced. Similarly, the time-frames which are applied to human economic life will need to be re-assessed. Most importantly, it will be necessary to escape from the chronic short-termism now common in business, government, industry and education.

The default notion of 'the present' which has dominated the industrial era has been a minimal and unlivable one: the fleeting present. Instead of accepting this passively, we need to get into the habit of consciously choosing appropriate time frames for different purposes. For some activities, such as typing, driving or playing music, a short time frame is vital. For others, such as listening to music, writing a story or resting, a longer one is needed. At the social and cultural level we should be thinking in decades and centuries. It is in the latter context that sustainability becomes an issue. So there is something of a chicken-and-egg problem here. Longer time frames legitimise the idea of sustainability; the latter also requires the former.

So it is important that several developments are seen together: a critique of industrial era economics, the rise of a different time sense and the implementation of a range of conserving measures and practices all reinforce each other in the longer term.

RELEASING THE POTENTIAL WITHIN PEOPLE

It was Schumacher who observed that, at the level of human beings, no upper limit to capacity can be found (Schumacher, 1977). This is so because we have evidence from many cultures and traditions that higher states of knowing and being have been achieved by outstanding individuals for many centuries. The work of writers such as Huxley, as well as the work of transpersonal psychologists, has done much to clarify the picture (Huxley 1945). So, in contrast to the usual machine-led view of the future, we can see a more humanly-compelling option taking shape. Essentially it is one in which *human* development accelerates to the point where it can assert dominance over *technical* development. That is the real challenge of the next century and beyond. If base human motives such as greed, fear, arrogance etc. continue to be linked with powerful technologies it is not hard to see the future as a continuing disaster.

Yet there exist within each culture all the potentials needed to empower other lines of development. They are accessible through clarity of insight, through deepened perception, creativity and certain forms of spiritual practice. *All reveal new possibilities precisely because they progressively refine the instrument of knowing itself.* As the latter changes, so does the wider world of which it is the most highly developed part. This is a principle of great, largely untapped, power.

Though it has been widely overlooked there remains a persistent thread throughout most cultures and spiritual traditions which suggests that we are all and always immersed in a stream of knowing in a world brimming with immanent meaning. Since language cannot fully encompass those realms, the descriptions may appear paradoxical. From within the desert of scientific empiricism that is the end of the story. But the account given above suggests that in any particular context the higher may not be *noticed* from within the lower and certainly cannot be explained by it. Thus, far from sustaining an adequate worldview, the tired rationalism now solidly embodied in educational, social, political and economic discourse around the world, itself represents a radically limited frame to read upon an interconnected world rich in hierarchical truths.

Higher awareness is refined, peaceful, compassionate. It is not under threat. It does not need to consume the world nor destroy it. It recognises, with Siddhartha, that 'meaning and reality (are) not hidden somewhere behind things, they (are) in them, in all of them' (Hesse 1951). The widespread recognition of such insights will not be quickly achieved. It is a distant goal. Yet the lines of development which it implies can energise very many changes in the here-and-now. The structures discussed above are steps on a long journey. It is a journey which leads up and out of the abyss toward new stages of personal and cultural development.

Here, then, is a key to cultural renewal and a renewed sense of meaning and purpose for the next century. For all persons have within them enormous capacities and powers which are hardly engaged in everyday life. Those who are able to locate their potential and to develop it have the ability to become constructive agents of change. The whole history of citizen action movements, of innovators and social activists tells us that people can indeed be very powerful. When linked with the right ideas and proposals this force is irresistable.

FINDING NEW PURPOSES AND MEANINGS

The purposes and meanings which powered the social system over some two hundred years have created a world of contradictions. The process of selecting new ones will not be an easy one since powerful groups always have interests bound up in the way things were. Yet the de-legitimisation of redundant social principles and practices is overdue. It begins with the critique of what is wrong, redundant, no longer helpful in contemporary cultures. It is a necessary ground-clearing exercise. It proceeds to develop alternative ways of knowing and being. These alternatives thrive upon new purposes and meanings, examples of which have been given above. Let us briefly consider three: stewardship, selfless love, and obligations to future generations.

A stewardship ethic could well be a motivating force in the establishment of new intentional communities which will spring up in formerly ravaged areas. Such communities will not be like the self-indulgent communes of the 1960s. Rather, they will exist to repair landscapes and re-invigorate ecosystems. They will be part of a shift toward long-term responsibility for the well-being of the earth.

Selfless love will be part of a shift away from the me-ness and materialism of the 20th century. It reflects an established trend from outer-directedness to inner-directness, or, from having to being (Fromm 1978). This is an important distinction. The having mode is insecure, needing constant reassurance and material inputs. On the contrary, the being mode is self-sufficient. It is centered in 'that which is' and sees the material realm as only one among others.

Obligations to future generations will emerge as a new (or renewed) social/cultural concern (Busuttil, 1990). Humans will no longer see themselves as cut off from past and future, but as participating in a cosmic process with no discernable beginning or end. In that process the generations are partners in time, each contributing to the overall journey.

Such developments will be supported by changes in worldviews which reveal the interwoven, interconnected, layering of reality. The latter will no longer be seen to reside primarily in material objects and physical powers, but will embrace other domains: emotional, mental and spiritual (Wilber, 1983, 1990).

THE REDISCOVERY OF INTRINSIC VALUE

It seems clear that present-day negative views of futures are driven by fairly primitive human instincts which are magnified and augmented by powerful technologies (particularly tools of communication and the mass media). The interaction of an industrial worldview with the political and commercial opportunism of the 20th century has permitted a crass, short-sighted marketing culture to become dominant. So it's hardly surprising that a positive view of the future is lost. It cannot be overemphasised that *the simple extension of present trends leads inexorably on to a devastated and impoverished world.* That fact underlies all the reasons why young people get depressed and makes it clear why business-as-usual assumptions are no longer viable. We are caught up in a giddy pattern of dynamic change and chronic unsolved world problems.

Yet it is entirely possible to 'breach the bounds' of present social reality and to imagine a very different world structured according to different values and assumptions. This could be the role of a 'wise culture' (Slaughter, 1991). It may not be achieved tomorrow, next year or even next century. What it does do is much more immediate and practical. It creates a contrast which, like the best speculative fiction, de-familiarises the present, makes it seem strange (ie. historically contingent). A compelling vision therefore appears which transcends the catastrophic futures endemic to technocratic scenarios.

How can one define a wise culture? We cannot be entirely sure. Perhaps the actual details are less important than *the quality of consciousness* which they evoke, for it is this which is arguably the pivot, rather than the technical or other means by which it is expressed. Nor need this quality be wholly displaced into future time. *The startling thing is that people have always been capable of it.* Today one such person may be Thomas Berry. His *The Dream of the Earth* seems to presage exactly the kind of shifts outlined here. Following Berman (whose book, *The Re-enchantment of the World* is a milestone in this literature) he writes,

> This re-enchantment with the earth as a living reality is the condition for our rescue of the earth from the impending destruction that we are imposing upon it. To carry this out effectively, we must now, in a sense, reinvent the human species within the community of life species. Our sense of reality and of value must consciously shift from an anthropocentric to a biocentric norm of reference . . . Our challenge is to create a new language, even a new sense of what it is to be human. It is to transcend not only national limitations, but even our species isolation, to enter the larger community of living species. This brings about a completely new sense of reality and value (Berry, 1988)

This 'new sense of reality and value' is, perhaps, the key to a new historical dynamic. In part it turns not on the intellectualization of experience, still less upon the reductionist interrogation of nature by naturalistic science; but rather upon *the direct experience of intrinsic value.* This stands in stark contrast to use-value and exchange-value which still remain core assumptions of the late industrial era. Imaging workshops which can bring participants to this point in living experience are clearly promoting social change at a very profound level.

Intrinsic value gives back to the earth, its wildlife and ecology the right to independent existence, regardless of the needs or uses of human kind. But, as McKibben and others have pointed out, from a human viewpoint nature can be said no longer to exist as an independent category. This may be overstated. Yet in order for nature to recover and retain its capacity to sustain any life it will need, in some sense, to be re-constituted at the heart of the social order.

RE-INVENTING CULTURE THROUGH A RENEWED WORLDVIEW

The way we see the world dictates the way we use it. So the commitments embedded in the foundations of industrial culture need to be examined and, where necessary, transformed or discarded. A renewed worldview will retain much that is good and useful from earlier times. It will retain notions of justice, equity and so on. But it will also include other elements such as sustainability, stewardship and a global, long-term view.

I have suggested that such a culture can arise from the inner dynamic of higher-order human capacities, founded on wisdom. But the fact is that no one really knows. The culture that follows on from industrialism cannot be specified fully in advance. What is certain is that if the human race is to survive in a world worth living in, a world rich in other life forms, rich in resources, rich in human and non-human options, then it will be with a culture based on assumptions very different than those now operating.

CONCLUSION: THE CHALLENGE AND PROMISE OF THE 21ST CENTURY

Possible futures for humankind are many and varied. The inert, radioactive desert is still a possibility, though less likely than it once was. More likely, at present is, a planet whose life-support systems are devastated beyond all hope of repair. In that scenario the four horsemen would ride at will across the densely-populated landscapes, wreaking their age-old havoc through famine, war, disease and pestilence. By contrast, there are some who place their hope on 'the high frontier', ie. the promise of space, orbiting colonies, mining the asteroids and so on. Others are unlocking the DNA code, pursuing nanotechnology and other such wonders. However, *the fatal flaw in many of these enterprises is that they leave the question of human motives unaddressed.*

As noted above, when primitive human instincts or motives such as fear, greed, hostility etc. become associated with powerful techno-logies, the result is, indeed, a long-running disaster. We have seen many of the latter in recent history. But when higher motives such as selfless love, stewardship and what Buddhists call 'loving kindness' come into play, there are interesting consequences (Macy, 1991). The grounds of many otherwise serious problems seem to disappear! Furthermore, many new technologies are seen to be unavoidably secondary. If they are applied at all then it is sparingly. Ethical concerns such as 'enoughness', a deep identification with the natural world and a developed interest in future generations come to the fore. In other words, *when a right relationship is re-established between people, culture and technology a whole new world of options emerges.*

This does not mean 'going back' to some pre-industrial condition of innocence, for in many ways we have as a species 'needed' the 20th century to make available to us certain kinds of experience, along with the experience of their costs and limitations. We have learned that the industrial assumptions about materialism, growth, the world as a machine or a resource and so on, are untenable. Consequently, we are challenged to create a new synthesis.

The promise of the 21st century lies in our ability to learn from the 20th and collectively to decide to strike out in new (or renewed) directions (Milbrath, 1989). In part, this means giving up the disastrous conceits of the past and embarking on a journey to explore the *heights* of human ability and potential. From that viewpoint, the future looks much less daunting.

THE BRINK OF MATURITY: TOWARDS A SCIENTIFIC MYTH OF OUR TIMES

Elisabet Sahtouris

We are very close to recognising that competition must be transformed into worldwide cooperation if we are to survive and mature as a species.

PARADOX

'A scientific myth' is apparently a paradox, for our contemporary industrial world culture holds science sacred and regards myth as the antithesis of science; as non-scientific illusion. Yet history shows that every human culture has had two ways of gaining knowledge and understanding of our place and role in nature and in the greater cosmos.

Simply put, they are the inner way and the outer way. The inner way encompasses intuition, dreaming, revelation, mythology; the outer, observation, experiment, reasoning, science. Very likely, we would not function well using only one or the other alone.

Great scientists and great Indian hunters alike first dream or intuit what they later carry out through observation and active test – and in doing so, they exemplify the full realisation of human potential. But while the Indian hunter is revered by his society for his ability to bring inner and outer knowledge together, and is expected to teach this way of life to others, the great scientist's inner experience is attributed to a 'quirk of genius' belonging solely to him, and to be kept strictly out of scientific (and more general) education.

The historic split between science and religion in our culture can be understood as reaction to the centuries in which religion was dominant and the Church suppressed science (and other religions) with fanatic zeal, from the destruction of the great library at Alexandria to repeated crusades against the 'Arab infidel' who guarded what was left of ancient scientific knowledge, the mass torture and execution of women practising natural medicine and the like treatment of Bruno and Galileo as heretics.

Science did not win its now dominant cultural position easily, and the scientific establishment had reason to guard against non-scientific ideas that were opposed to science. Yet while it has proved less vicious than the formerly dominant Church in suppressing competitive ideas, it has been equally self-righteous in professing 'the one true science' and equally thorough in expunging 'non-scientific' ideas and practices within its ranks and in denigrating them throughout its own and other cultures – non-scientific ideas being defined as everything identified above as inner knowledge and all outer knowledge gained within worldviews, theories or tests other than those officially recognized by the scientific establishment. Indigenous science, for example, is not recognized by the scientific establishment as science because it has not separated itself from sacred or inner knowledge.

Separation and integration are fundamental processes in nature – all things struggle for identity, yet all things are related and interdependent. Our contemporary industrial culture, however, is still confused on how aspects of culture can have their own identity, yet be harmoniously integrated. On the one hand we almost idolize cultures such as the ancient Greek and modern Balinese for their integration of art, science and the sacred; on the other we strongly resist such integration in our own culture.

Among this century's greatest scientific advances is the understanding of science itself as an evolving human endeavour within an historical context. In particular, philosophers of science have shown us that scientific worldviews – views of so-called 'reality' – are historically changing constructs – that the prevailing scientific paradigm of one era can be invalid in the next; that scientific theories can be judged only by experimental tests of their usefulness, not of their truth; that science is the endeavour to create maps to reality and differs from religion by constructing the maps rationally and refining them through experimental tests rather than accepting without question maps acquired by revelation.

These advances in scientific understanding have not been easy to put into scientific practice. It remains difficult to accept the implied uncertainty of scientific knowledge after taking such stock in its certainty. In fact, much scientific pronouncement and practice suggests that most scientists still hold science to be the ultimate arbiter of truth about our world. Despite resistance, however, the monolithic nature of the scientific establishment, and of its currently prevailing scientific paradigm, must be questioned in the light of the above discoveries about the nature of science itself. For these discoveries do not in any way dictate a single worldview or approach to science; on the contrary they suggest the possibility of alternative worldviews, theories and experimental tests, all within the realm of science.

A mechanical, scientific worldview, for example, may continue to be useful in creating new technology, but it fails us as a map to living as a healthy species in a healthy environment, even to choosing which technologies will serve that goal and which will not. Indigenous science are likely to be of more use for such purposes.

MYTHIC HERITAGE

As our new myths must continue or update the ongoing saga of humans in nature, let us begin with the heritage of old myth on which we must build. Choosing just two examples we find that native prophecies and classical Greek myths alike tell of the adventure of discovery and invention that part of humanity must pursue, and also of the drastic consequences to follow if this adventure leads to matlerialism and egotism rather than to reunion with nature in mature wisdom.

Hopi prophecy tells that red and white brothers were separated so the white brother could develop his powers to record and invent things while the red brother took care of the land in spiritual ways. It was intended that they would eventually reunite to join the material and spiritual worlds, and it was predicted that if the white brother turned away from these instructions, many troubles would develop.

In Greek myth, the hero must also leave home to develop and test his powers in the world, to face dangers and accomplish great deeds, but his mission was to return as a mature, wise man who could bring order to his home land. If his egotistic pride – *hubris* – led him to lose respect for the gods and fail to gain wisdom, he would fall and bring about disaster.

In these mythic traditions we can easily recognize the historic human adventure that has culminated in the modern industrial/ technological world: in the Greek myth, an heroic adventure fraught with danger from the outset, yet a natural expression, perhaps even an imperative, of our explorative, creative capacities; in the Hopi myth the adventure of the white brother has now brought all of us into such trouble that we are in danger of species extinction, while the red brother is that part of humanity we call indigenous people, who struggle to keep the land by sacred practice.

A few hundred years ago in the Renaissance, developing ideas that originated in ancient Greece, the white brother as white European separated himself from nature, developing an objective science based on his own inventions of mathematics and machinery, projecting them onto nature as a mechanical worldview that determined scientific practice and led to the development of modern industrial society.

Meanwhile, those indigenous cultures that survived the ruthless process of industrialisation, kept to the red brother's role of keeping the land by observing and keeping to the ways of nature in sacred practice. In terms of the Odysseus myth, this role is Penelope's, the faithful partner who 'kept the home fires burning'.

We are now at the turning point in both myths: where the white brother must choose between plunging all humanity into disaster or returning to seek the wisdom of the red brother to temper his knowledge and use it wisely, in harmony with the natural world; where the hero must overcome his ego to bring his experience to bear on a wise ordering of affairs upon his own return home, or suffer the consequences of his hubris. The grand adventure, in reality as in myth, has brought us to the choice between suicidal extinction or maturity as as species.

Our maturity depends on the reunion of white and red brothers, of Odysseus and Penelope, on tempering the adventurous experience of developing science and technology with wisdom born of familiarity with nature and on reverence for all life as sacred. New globally meaningful myths for our times will thus emerge as integrations of ancient myths and prophecies, indigenous practice and modern scientific understanding of our living planet in all its evolution.

NEW SCIENCE

The idea that we can find guidance for human affairs in the ways of nature was actually inherent in the roots of modern 'Western' science. The first Greek philosopher-scientists deliberately sought the order in living nature as a guiding source of order in human society. This perspective, however, was abandoned when the conception of humans as part of nature and of nature as alive was transformed into a conception of nature as mechanical and separate from humans. Then scientific endeavour became the search for ways to manipulate and control nature to human ends. Yet, to bring up paradox again, mechanistic science has now led us via space exploration to James Lovelock's Gaia theory that nature – in particular our planet as a whole – is, after all, alive. It is also the technology born of mechanical science, in its evident ravages upon nature, that is making us aware that we must change not only our worldview but our whole way of life.

A particularly fascinating revelation that struck me in my own study of 'Gaian' (live Earth) science, and which seems very relevant to creating a new guiding myth for our times, is that we humans are now reliving an evolutionary drama written by nature billions of years ago. In our Sun-star system, only the Earth came alive as solar and core energy transformed surface rock and water into living matter. The slow linear chemistry of geological weathering was transformed into the more energetic circular chemistry of metabolic organisms until the surface was literally crawling with tiny bacteria that, in turn, created the new chemistry of seas, atmosphere and soils, even reorganising minerals into pure veins.

These first creatures our own most remote ancestors, were, like ourselves, highly creative. Ancient bacteria, in fact, invented all the ways of making a living on this planet, and all sorts of technologies from microscopic electric motors and nuclear energy plants to that grand worldwide information exchange system we humans have just uncovered and called DNA recombination. But also like ourselves, they caused major environmental problems, even planetwide pollution of crisis proportions rivalling today's.

Their environmental crisis was caused by their massive production of the highly corrosive, deadly gas oxygen. Those bacteria that survived resolved the crisis by inventing a new way of life – they turned a bad thing into a good thing by using oxygen to make energy more efficiently than by their other methods: fermentation and photosynthesis. The new method, respiration, is the one we ourselves have inherited, for the descendants of the first respiring bacteria are the mitochondria that make our energy, residing in droves in all our cells, as well as in those of all other living creatures that are not themselves bacteria: all protists, fungi, plants and animals.

The link between ancient bacteria and ourselves I see as a drama that begins at a stage of life when bacteria, still the only organisms on Earth, were engaged in a kind of imperialism or system of colonization. The more energetic respiring and photosynthetic bacteria were invading and colonizing larger and, we might say, less developed fermenting bacteria, ruthlessly exploiting their 'resources', leaving them weak and helpless, if not dead.

Eventually however, this competitive, exploitative way of life that led only to dead ends for exploiters and exploited alike, was transformed into a new cooperative way of life. In that process, exploiters and exploited living together as colonies formed themselves into huge (for the time) new cells with a cooperative division of labour and nuclei composed of their shared DNA.

This stage of Earth's evolution, when bacterial cells united into nucleated cells was so significant that we may well see it as the greatest step in all evolution up to the present, because every living thing of Earth larger than bacteria is fundamentally one such cell. Many species, including our own, clone elaborate multi-celled bodies from that initial cell in each generation, thereby producing huge organisms: no multi-celled organisms, including humans, can exist without having gone through that single cell stage. Our evolutionary connections are such that biologically we are vast colonies of cloned bacterial cooperatives descended from the ancient ones described here. We are repeating the same behavioural struggle of our ancient ancestral bacteria in trying to transform our competitive and exploitative way of life into healthy cooperation. Though we have still to learn many details of their social structure's transformation, we do know that before the ancient bacteria built the great cooperatives of which our bodies are made, they invented technologies of chemical communication, physical transportation, and complex information systems, all on a microscopic level that we are only now able to understand through our own modern technology.

RESOLUTION

The timing of this new knowledge is most interesting, because the story of cell evolution we are just learning is so very like our present world situation. In the process of human imperialistic adventures, colonial exploitation and other forms of economic competition, we, like the bacteria, have developed extensive transport, communications and information systems, now available to cooperative use. Neither the ancient bacteria nor modern humans developed such systems in order to unite themselves, but such is the logic or order of nature that systems under stress must reorganize themselves using whatever means are at their disposal to become healthy or they die out.

We are very close to recognizing that competition must be transformed into worldwide cooperation if we are to survive and mature as a species. When we take this imminent evolutionary step of uniting humanity, we will have no choice but to follow this natural order. In terms of the myths, the white brother of industrial society clearly must abandon his notion that material wealth is the road to happiness, that national product is the measure of progress, and that hostile competition is the way of nature. He must, in short, relearn the cooperative ways of nature from his own new scientific knowledge and from his red brother, whose science of nature is older, yet in some ways more advanced.

Indigenous science, in conjunction with sacred practice, is not aimed at 'progress' but at 'right living'. Among native Americans and many other indigenous cultures, the central tenet is reverence for all life and the responsibility for its wellbeing. In these matters the white brother must cease to destroy and learn to respect, preserve and look for guidance to those red brother cultures that have stayed in touch with the natural world, knowing its ways intimately, following them by practising an ethic of sharing rather than accumulation. The past half millennium is soon to be celebrated for Columbus' 'discovery' of America at its onset. Yet as history continues to reveal itself, especially through the work of Harvard professor Barry Fell (Fell 1978 & 1980) and his growing number of colleagues, red indigenous and white European trading or immigrant cultures were peacefully integrated in the Americas again and again from pre-Christian times to the Spanish conquest, leaving countless artifacts and linguistic records that have until recently been indecipherable or misunderstood. In fact, this integration, followed by as yet unknown incidents of white men's departures from the Americas, may well lie behind the beautiful legend of Quetzalcoatl as a white man who would return from the sea, the hospitable Aztec welcome betrayed by the Spanish conquistadors, and perhaps the Hopi myth of the red and white brothers.

The new guiding myths for our times, then, will portray visions of humanity coming out of crisis and into mature, wise harmony – native and industrialized peoples respecting each other's diversity as they unite efforts to integrate the best of all their cultures in humility and respect.

THE SECOND SCIENTIFIC REVOLUTION

Willis Harman

'Looking to . . . the cultural shift, what seems evident is that close to the heart of it is a new sense of holism, of everything connected to everything . . . Whatever the anticipated "new paradigm" turns out to be, this sense of wholeness seems clearly to be a part of it. . . .'

In his *Introduction to Metaphysics* the eminent French philosopher Henri Bergson said of the 'much-desired union of science and metaphysics' that it would 'lead the positive sciences, properly so-called, to become conscious of their true scope, . . . far greater than they imagine.' (Bergson 1974) I have come to believe that the time for realization of that dream has arrived, and that this union, which I expect to be consummated early in the 21st century, will be judged by future historians to be as consequential as was the scientific revolution of the 17th century – and that, as we know, changed *everything*.

As a matter of fact, it might be more accurate to speak instead of the *reunion* of science and metaphysics, for throughout the early history of science the two were strongly linked. The Royal Society, founded in 1660, greatly influenced the early development of science; during this early period science and metaphysics were so intertwined as to be two aspects of a single endeavour. The founders of the Royal Society, including Robert Boyle and Sir Christopher Wren, the first President, Robert Moray, and Sir Isaac Newton, President of the Royal Society from 1703 to 1727, were all steeped in the esoteric metaphysical traditions of Freemasonry, Rosicrucian, Neo-Platonic, and Hermetic thought.

The word 'metaphysics' has two quite different meanings in common usage. The first meaning is a branch of philosophy comprising mainly *ontology*, dealing with the question 'What is the nature of ultimate reality?' and *epistemology*, concerned with the question 'How do you know?'. The second meaning is the study of the transcendent or supersensible, the contacting of the reality that lies 'beyond the physical.' It is the second sense to which Bergson was referring in his statement, and to which the early members of the Royal Society were aligned. But for the union to take place, it turns out to be necessary to re-examine the metaphysical (first sense) assumptions underlying modern science.

Two competing pictures of reality.   Western culture has for a long time been trying to manage a society based on two incompatible pictures of reality – one 'scientific' and the other in some sense 'spiritual.' The former tended to deny the spiritual, and the latter found science irrelevant to the important questions of life. British author C.P. Snow wrote about the phenomenon in a much-quoted 1959 book *Two Cultures*. The scientific worldview was, and is, powerfully influential in the political, economic, and industrial institutions of modern society. However, people have tended to live their lives by, and society to derive its values from, the other, competing worldview. Since the two worldviews are incompatible and imply quite different approaches to life, it is not surprising that by the end of the 20th century the long-term viability of 'two-cultures' society was seriously in question. (Snow 1959)

For an assortment of pragmatic and political reasons, Western science by the 18th century had adopted *an ontological assumption of separateness:* separability of observer from observed; of man from nature; of mind from matter; of science from religion; separateness of 'fundamental particles' from one another; separability of the parts of a system or organism to understand how it 'really' works; separateness of scientific disciplines; of investigators, competing over who made a discovery first.

This assumption of separateness leads to the hubris that humankind can pursue its own objectives as though the Earth and the other creatures are here for its benefit; to the myth of the 'objective observer'; to reductionist explanations; to the ethic of competition. It implies the locality of causes; that is, it precludes 'action at a distance,' either in space or time. It implies the *epistemological assumption that our sole empirical basis for constructing a science is the data from our physical senses.*

From these two metaphysical assumptions follow the premises of logical empiricism which are typically taken to be intrinsic to modern science – objectivism, positivism, reductionism. By the middle of this century there was almost complete consensus that these are the proper foundation assumptions for science. They amount to the premise that the basic stuff of the universe is precisely what physicists study: namely, matter and physical energy – ultimately, 'fundamental particles,' their associated fields and interrelationships.

An alternate set of assumptions.   Scientists typically take these ontological and epistemological postulates to be inviolate, to be an inherent and ineluctable part of the definition of science. To be sure, these foundation assumptions have been modified with the advent of quantum physics, particularly by the indeterminacy principle and the inherent statistical nature of measurement of the very small. But the 'second scientific revolution' involves far more fundamental change – actual replacement of these underlying premises by dramatically different assertions.

Agreement is spreading that science must develop the ability to look at things, particularly living things, more holistically. An ontological assumption that everything experienced – including both physical and mental – is part of an intercommunicating unity, a oneness, is supported by at least as much experiential evidence as that used to justify an assumption of separateness. In such a wholeness view, it is only when a part of the whole can be sufficiently isolated from the rest that reductionistic causes *appear* to describe adequately why things behave as they do, and the ordinary concepts of scientific causation apply.

Dr. Lynn Magulis, Professor of Botany at the University of Massachusetts at Amherst, told an audience at the 1991 annual meeting of the American Association for the Advancement of Science that bacteria and other one-celled animals react as though they involve something akin to consciousness in the human being. If something like consciousness is to be found in all living organisms, is it utterly preposterous to postulate a substratum of consciousness pervading the entire physical universe? Or for that matter, a superstratum?

One of the main implications of a science based on the premise of an ultimate oneness is the epistemological assertion that we contact reality in not one, but two ways. One of these is through physical sense data – which form the basis of normal science. The other is through being ourselves part of the oneness – through a deep intuitive 'inner knowing.' Putting it another way, the epistemological tissue involved is whether our encountering a reality is limited to being aware of, and giving meaning to, the messages from our physical senses (typically approvingly referred to as 'objective'), or whether it includes also a subjective aspect in an intuitive, aesthetic, spiritual, noetic and mystical sense. (An often overlooked intuitive and aesthetic factor has always been present in science – for example, in the aesthetic principle of 'elegance'; in the 'principle of parsimony' for choosing between alternative explanations; even in distinguishing what are 'phenomena' or 'data' from the background which simply goes unnoticed.)

The restructuring of science.   This, then, is the restructuring of science that comprises the 'second scientific revolution' – restructuring on the basis of an *ontological assumption of oneness and wholeness,* and an *epistemological choice to include as input both physical sense data and subjective experience,* in particular the experience of such trained 'inner explorers' as are found in the various esoteric and spiritual traditions. Of course, scientists are hesitant to consider such a radical restructuring of science if some lesser measure would suffice to accommodate all of the known characteristics of consciousness and the related 'anomalies.'. However, by the end of the 20th century it was becoming apparent to many scientists that replacing 'separateness-based' science with an 'extended' wholeness-based science would solve some basic puzzles relating to consciousness and would meet many of the criteria of earlier attempts to reform science. It would not invalidate any of the physical and biological science built up over several centuries; it would simply be more inclusive.

This restructured and 'extended' science includes and emphasises *more participatory methodologies;* it assumes that, whereas we learn certain kinds of things by distancing ourselves from the object under scrutiny, we get another kind of knowledge from intuitively 'becoming one with' that which is being studied.

Secondly, it favours *more holistic and organismic models in the biological and human sciences;* it is not reductionist in any dogmatic sense. The biological sciences involve holistic concepts (e.g. organism, function of an organ) which have no counterparts in, and are not reducible to, the physical sciences. Similarly, there is no reason to assume that the characteristics of consciousness are reducible to biology. In other words, while theory reduction (as, for example, the laws of optics explained through electromagnetic theory) will be welcomed whenever it proves to be possible, it is not a dogma of this science that it must be, in general, possible.

And thirdly, it *emphasizes subjective experience* as a valid 'window' through which to explore certain aspects of reality. It includes, in addition to the reductionistic 'upward causation' which presently dominates the scientific world, a further concept of 'downward causation,' or causation-from-consciousness. Since consciousness and purpose are found in some part of the oneness that is the universe (namely, human beings), they are by virtue of that fact characteristic of the universe as a whole. Thus conscious awareness, unconscious processes, intention, volition, and the concept of the self, are not, in this extended science, 'anomalies'; they are simply aspects of the universe to be explored. It follows that there is no fundamental inconsistency between science and the recommendation, in the 'perennial wisdom' of the world's spiritual traditions, of an inner search involving some sort of meditative or yogic discipline, and discovery of and identification with, a 'higher' or 'true' Self which is beyond the physical realm but is nevertheless real.

Evolution in the 'oneness' picture. In the neo-Darwinian concept of evolution, the organism and its environment have separate existences; although both change, they do so through their own separate processes. The outlook of 'extended' science leads to a more dialectical view in which organisms are both the subjects and objects of evolution: they both make and are made by the environment and are thus actors in their own revolutionary history. The most striking example is the conversion, around two billion years ago by living organisms themselves, of the reducing atmosphere that existed before the beginning of life to one that is rich in reactive oxygen. James Lovelock has given many other examples in justifying his 'Gaia' concept of the earth as a living organism. (Lovelock, 1979)

Furthermore, since consciousness is a characteristic of the universe, there is no reason to assume other than that it has been present throughout evolution. In the neo-Darwinian thesis, human consciousness is assumed to have biologically emerged from animal consciousness. But in the 'oneness' view, as Owen Barfield has put it, consciousness 'is the inner side of the whole, just as human consciousness is the inside of one human being. . . . Once you have realised that there is indeed only one world, though with both an inside and an outside to it, only one world experienced by our senses from without, and by our consciousness from within, . . . it is no longer possible to separate evolution from evolution of consciousness.' (Barfield 1985)

In this view there is one universe, evolving, with the individual human observer as part of the whole. Thus, any concept of reality based on the idea of an 'objective scientific observer' is suspect. Whatever perception of reality is arrived at by the scientist, it is a consequence of the interaction of perceiving organism and environment as they have evolved together.

Further characteristics of an 'extended' science.   In the process of research guided by a 'oneness' concept of the universe, the experience of observing brings about sensitization and other changes in the observer. Thus *a willingness to be transformed* himself or herself is an essential characteristic of the participatory scientist. The anthropologist who wishes to truly understand a culture other than her own must allow that experience to change her so that the new culture is seen through new eyes, not eyes conditioned by her own culture. The psychotherapist who would perceive his client without distortion must have worked through his own neuroses which would otherwise warp perception. So, the scientist who wants to study, for example, meditative processes and the transcendent experiences so treasured in the various spiritual traditions, has to be willing to go through the deep changes which will make him or her a competent observer.

To some, the idea of an 'extended' science is likely to appear regressive, risking a re-opening of the door to dogmas and superstitions of past ages. But openness to alternative theories and explanations, and healthy scepticism, are at least as important in this extended science as they are in present science. Consensual validation of findings also remains of central importance, but it is accomplished in a somewhat different way.

The phenomena and experiences which are typically considered 'paranormal' with respect to present science, fit comfortably in such a restructured science. Not that all reports of such phenomena are accurate; it is simply that they are not ruled out *a priori* by a hidden ontological premise. In other words, what is considered 'anomalous' or 'paranormal' is a matter of choice of the foundation assumptions of science.

The significance of the 'second scientific revolution.'   It has been a crucial mistake of modern society to assume that ultimately, positivistic reductionistic 'scientific' causes can explain everything. That view led to unsolvable paradoxes like 'free will versus determinism,' 'the mind-body problem,' and 'science versus religion.' It led to our denying the validity of our deepest feelings, value commitments, and spiritual insight. We look forward now, as we approach the 21st century, to a more complete science in which nothing of human experience is excluded by the tyranny of founding philosophical assumptions which masquerade as ineluctable axioms or valid scientific findings.

I feel the need to emphasize again that shifting the metaphysical foundations of science as postulated above in no way invalidates most of the scientific knowledge that has been built up over the centuries. The knowledge of present science is still valid; but it is placed in a different context, and interpreted differently. Present reductionistic science will still be available for the purposes to which it is suited, namely generation of technologies for manipulation of the physical world, and understanding regular aspects of that world. But that kind of science will no longer have the authority to insist that we humans are here, solely through random causes, in a meaningless universe; nor that our consciousness is 'merely' the chemical and physical processes of the brain.

The scientific revolution of the 17th century, which was really a shift in the dominant picture of reality, marked the end of the Middle Ages and the beginning of modern times – an era characterized by growing dominance of materialistic values; technical and economic logic; scientific, industrial and economic institutions. The 'second scientific revolution' denotes another fundamental shift in the dominant picture of reality; a shift toward a view in which the universe is fundamentally alive and imbued with purpose, understanding comes from both 'inner' and 'outer' experience, and our relationship to the whole is one of deep involvement and co-creation. It marks the beginning of a new era; a new era full of promise because although severe global problems remain, their origins are in the reality picture of the era being left behind, and the characteristics of the new reality picture render their solution possible.

EARTH MIGHT BE FAIR

James Ogilvy

'Simply to be a human being is to be a futurist of sorts. For human freedom is largely a matter of imagining alternative futures and then choosing among them.'

Despite my own postmodern waverings between secular atheism and pagan polytheism, I am nonetheless drawn to the sheer poetry of the Christian hymns I was forced to sing in compulsory chapel at school. 'Earth might be fair and all men glad and wise . . . ' What a wonderful idea, even in its sexist formulation. 'All persons glad and wise,' wouldn't exactly scan.

Earth might be fair: the richness lies precisely in the ambiguity as between ethical and aesthetic interpretations of 'fair.' We could certainly do with a little more justice; and we could also do with more beauty, the Shakespearean meaning of 'fair.'

Imagine a world without lawyers, a world where disputes did not have to be settled in court because there were so many fewer disputes to begin with. Imagine a world where generosity and goodwill were the norm rather than suspicion and defensiveness. Imagine a world where all the resources now devoted to processing and adjudicating insurance claims were instead devoted to preventive health maintenance. Imagine a world where all the resources now devoted to advertising were instead devoted to quality improvements in products. Just as we are now learning to live in a world where the Cold War is over and we can entertain the distribution of a peace dividend, imagine a time when we could entertain the distribution of a litigation dividend, an insurance dividend, an advertising dividend.

But what would all the lawyers and insurance salesmen and advertising copywriters *do*? What will all the Russian soldiers do? But is it any justification for existing practices that place a high burden on other human beings that the human beings who practise them don't have anything else to do? Let them play. I'm serious. Let me explain.

One of the problems of a postmodern economy is to find alternatives to the industrious productivity of work as a measure of economic health. What if we are working to produce too much of the wrong stuff? Throughout pre-modern and modern times, productivity was a legitimate measure of economic strength. People did not have enough of the basic necessities and we depended on natural science and technology to improve our ability to get more out of less in less time. But now there is general agreement among the technoelite that the remaining pockets of hunger are caused not by a lack of agricultural capacity, but by social and political snafus that leave food rotting in the field; homelessness is caused not by the lack of raw materials for dwellings, but by policies that force foreclosures on people who cannot cope with the complexities of global economy.

At risk of gross over-simplification I want to say that our most vexing problems today are not problems that can be solved by science and technology; they are human problems that call for a degree of social invention that we have not seen since the creation of democracy and the writing of the Constitution. We don't yet know how to organize our human interactions. Some of us haven't even learned how to play together; or if we have, we've grown up and forgotten. Consequently we try to make up for a lack of joy by enjoying the material possessions that science and technology and the market economy can spew forth with abandon.

Take the nuclear family, one of the principal means of organising human interactions. Recall poet Philip Larkin's famous line: 'They fuck you up, your mum and dad.' But they had their problems too: Victorian upbringing, a culture of possessive individualism that has evolved from what social critics called alienation to what a more psychoanalytically oriented critique calls narcissism-learning to live with alienation and love it by loving only oneself.

Surely there must be a better way to raise hairless monkeys. But what might it be? Maybe if mom and dad were less alienated, less over-worked, less tired at the end of the day . . . then earth might be fair. If more fathers and mothers raised children who retained a sense of wonder, and a sense of humour; if mom and dad could avoid the descent of their own love into squabbles over what he said she said about what he did . . . then earth might be fair. But until then we will remain locked in the same old Freudian/Frankfurt School family drama that extends from exploitation in the workplace to oppression over the breakfast table . . . if there is a breakfast table and not a staggered grabbing for Fruit Loops and Pop Tarts on the way to work.

Despite the wonders of modern science there never seems to be enough: enough love, enough attention, enough respect, enough dignity. So we make too much of the things we know how to make: war, toxic wastes, bad television. Perhaps there is a better way to organize our lives and our relationships, one that does not pit the demands of work against the delights of love. Perhaps there is a way to reconstruct our world. But in doing so we cannot base our reconstruction on the firm foundations of science. Nor will we be able to depend on transcendent norms as a measure of the better. Instead, like sailors rebuilding our ship at sea, we must fashion our new world from what we have at hand: our existing legal system, our existing healthcare system, our existing educational system, our existing families. So the job is not altogether utopian.

But let us not forget that radical change for the better *is* possible. Dictatorships in Haiti, the Philippines and Nicaragua *have* been toppled in the last decade – which is not to say that their successors are without problems. Real per capita disposable income in the United States *has* grown over ten-fold in the twentieth century – which is not to say that we know what to do with the money. Nor should we ignore real declines in the same figure over the past fifteen years for the lower quintiles of the population. Finally and most emphatically, the fall of the Iron Curtain and the end of the Cold War must offer lessons of hope regarding other seemingly intractable issues.

I can recall spending a week at a retreat in Wyoming with a very brainy group from the John F. Kennedy School at Harvard, plus assembled experts like Robert MacNamara, Representative Les Aspin, and a former Ambassador to Austria, all gathered in the early 1980s to entertain alternatives to nuclear deterrence fifty years into the future. I had been asked to help with the methodology of alternative scenario development. But in the course of five days of intense discussion I was unable to bend the collective wisdom of that group to entertain seriously any scenario that would contain less then 50% of the then current force structure over the next fifty years – still enough megatons to make the rubble bounce and render the earth uninhabitable. Less than ten years later we now take for granted what was then unthinkable to some very good thinkers. Surely there is a lesson here somewhere about the impotence of hope among intellectuals when confronted by the power of entrenched acceptance of the intolerable. We intellectuals would err on the side of pessimism rather than be accused of naiveté. World-weary pessimism seems so much more intellectually respectable than even the best educated hope.

But I would argue that the fashionable face of all-knowing despair is finally immoral. Granted, the bubble-headed optimism of Pangloss and Polyanna are equally immoral. A refusal to look at poverty or oppression can contribute to their perpetuation; but so can an intellectual commitment to their inevitability.

So let us entertain, at least for a moment, a scenario that builds on what we are learning from the human sciences – a scenario that exhibits some of the features of an emergent paradigm. Imagine, if you will, *sublimation of the economy*. In fact it is already happening if you can see it as such. The industrial economy of the production and consumption of material things is giving way to an information economy of ephemeral entertainments and services. This is not news. But the *interpretation* of this epochal shift in the way we earn our daily bread has not yet been fully developed in terms of the Semiotic Turn[1] evident in the human sciences. Instead the slogan, *All that is solid melts into air*, has been interpreted, from Karl Marx to Marshall Berman[2] as a lament over the loss of normative meaning that the process of modernisation has wreaked upon stable cultures. But once we decouple the normative from the eternal, once we fully accept *the fall into time*[3] then there is a possibility – worth entertaining as one among several scenarios – that the statement, *All that is solid melts into*

[1]   The phrase, 'the Semiotic Turn,' refers to a broad shift in the human sciences, from anthropology and psychology to philosophy and literary criticism. In each of these disciplines there has been a retreat from a positivism that would reduce symbols to a physicalistic explanation of signification. Instead, the new understanding of signs – from words to clothes and other status symbols – sees the semiotic realm as an autonomous and irreducible domain for the interpretation of meanings, not the measurement of facts.

[2]   Cf. Marshall Berman, *All That is Solid Melts into Air,* New York, Simon & Schuster, 1982, especially Part II.1, 'The Melting Vision and its Dialectic.' Berman takes his title from Marx's formulation in *The Communist Manifesto*.

[3]   'The fall into time' refers to the embrace of historicity since Hegel. Unlike Plato, for whom 'time is the moving image of eternity,' post-Hegelian thinkers – from Marx and Nietzsche to Heidegger and Michel Foucault – acknowledge the historical development of a series of forms of consciousness. This historicity of consciousness cuts us off from any once-and-for-all access to timeless universals or absolute truths. For a fuller explication of both the Semiotic Turn and the Fall into Time, see the much longer version of the present paper published in *Futures Research Quarterly (1992)*.

air, might cease to be interpreted as a lament for lost certainties and become instead an announcement of the advent of the sublime.

Sublimatio was the term the alchemists used for the process by which the philosopher's stone was heated to a point where it melted into vapour – air – without ever passing through the intermediate liquid state. Sublimation was later taken by Freud to mean the process by which erotic and aggressive instincts are redirected into the creation of art, culture and religion – thus allowing him, under the influence of a mechanistic-physicalistic paradigm, to then *reduce* the products of culture to *nothing but* redirected instinctual energy – art as so much smeared shit. But the metaphor of sublimation – and, like the alchemists, I take it only as a metaphor – can just as well be taken as an access to the sublime. When the mechanistic-physicalistic paradigm is shifted by the Semiotic Turn, then there is an opportunity for reinterpreting the efficacy of the sublime *all the way down* rather than reducing culture to the redirection of base instincts all the way up.

In talking this way about the sublime, I know I risk gaining allies I don't want. I do not want the support of New Age enthusiasts who think that the sublime is some esoteric realm that can be accessed by incantations, crystals, or yet another seminar on the Course in Miracles. Nor do I hope to please supporters of that ole' time religion. Virtually every form of orthodox religion – with the possible exception of Zen Buddhism, whose supporters deny that it is a religion – seem to me to be subject to charges of childishness, wish fulfilment, and an indulgence in magical thinking that is inconsistent with the real contributions that science has made to our interaction with our environment. Whatever religions may have contributed to social organization and psychological well-being in the pre-modern world, in our postmodern world their muiltiplicity means that they are in danger of doing more harm than good. We don't need more *jihads*.

No, the process of sublimation we are now undergoing owes little or nothing to an already completed, eternal sublime. Nor can it be reduced to a redirection of instinctual or material foundations. Instead it is a self-referential, emergent, creative lifting by the bootstraps that generates meaning *where there was none*. It is not impossible, nor are there any guarantees. This is the bane and the blessing of human freedom in the realm of the sublime.

Imagine a scenario in which educational reform were finally taken seriously, not as the imposition of some new religion on the young, but as the cultivation of human potential. The tools are at hand, but today we have not yet applied those tools in our schools. Instead we expose our children to teachers who are drawn from the lowest quintile of our universities' graduating classes. As they say, those that can, do; those that can't, teach. But imagine what could happen if education became the cause of the nineties, much as civil rights and the Vietnam war preoccupied the sixties, or feminism and the environment motivated so many in the seventies, or greed obsessed the eighties. It could happen. Social agendas do change.

If education became the cause of the nineties, if teachers' salaries were raised and the respect paid to educators enhanced, then by the turn of the century we might be graduating students who were truly skilful, not just in the manufacture of physical goods, but in the creation and consumption of the sublime. And how much lighter on the earth such an economy would be!

The spread of industrial manufacturing to produce more *things* puts our environment at severe risk. This is not news. But only now are we beginning to see that economic growth need not be correlated with energy demand or the exploitation of non-renewable resources. In our work with one of the nation's largest electric utility companies, Pacific Gas and Electric, Global Business Network has helped fashion scenarios that show PG&E's future as dependent not on generating and selling *more* energy, but on building profitability by helping their consumers consume *less* energy. PG&E can sell what Amory Lovins calls *negawatts* rather than megawatts. PG&E can sell conservation and still stay in business. Paradigm shifts are possible, even for upper management.

Better education can lead to more efficient use of energy. And there are technologies under development that can help clean up the mess we have already made. Nanotechnology – the technology of manufacturing at the molecular level – may be able to generate mini-machines that eat toxic wastes or transform them into useful resources. It is possible, according to Eric Drexler, author of *Engines of Creation*. The possibilities were at least sufficiently intriguing to motivate Global Business Network to host the first international conference on nanotechnology.

Bio-technology promises similar breakthroughs. Of course it is possible that we will release some horrible mutation on the face of the earth. Negative scenarios must be developed as cautionary tales. There is a Faustian hubris to scenarios that depend solely on techno-fixes. But there are some techno-fixes that will be required if this scenario is to advance from its beginning through its middle toward an end.

If this scenario's beginning depends on vast improvements in our educational system, it's middle would chart the application of intelligence to many of our more or less technical problems: energy, the health of the environment, the health of individuals. There are feedback loops in this scenario, vicious circles that turn virtuous. Today too many children show up at school too sick and malnourished to learn anything at all. Tomorrow's students might be better fed, healthier, and therefore better able to learn how to stay healthy. It is possible.

It is also possible that the sublimation of the economy will lighten the burden on the earth that our industrial economy creates in the first place. *Pace* Paul and Anne Ehrlich, who trace most of the earth's ills to over-population, perhaps a human species less bent on material possessions and material consumption might be able to raise rather than lower the carrying capacity of the ecosphere. In order to contemplate such a scenario one must pass through a paradigm shift from a mechanistic-energetic physics of reality, through the Semiotic Turn, to the economics of the sublime. For only on the other side of that paradigm shift does one begin to escape the law of the constant conservation of matter and energy. So I want to return to the centrality of the Semiotic Turn as an interpretation of the information revolution, and to the Fall into Time as an aspect of our self-understanding of human freedom.

I know of no law of the constant conservation of laughter, or any limitation on joy. I see no reason to limit our sense of what is possible for the distribution of delight. These human *goods* need not be subject to a law of constant conservation. If I have more, you needn't have less. Quite to the contrary, there might be a virtuous circle of mutual reinforcement in the spread of sublime delight, like a ripple of laughter that gains momentum in a crowd. According to the economics of the sublime, there *can* be *enough* for all.

I know that this scenario is beginning to sound impossibly utopian, like something sprouted from the shores of California where the loco-weed grows. So I will hasten to add something about the problems that have *not* been solved by the middle of this scenario.

There is no universal understanding of the best way to live a deeply fulfilling human life. On the contrary there is a rich and variegated ecology of customs and mores. Further, there is a constant risk of *transgression*. Precisely to the extent that people have learned that *being good* is not necessarily about conforming to timeless norms, but rather more about exercising human freedom in the service of creativity and delight, there is a constant danger of decadence. For like creativity in art, creativity in life sometimes requires a bending of the rules for the sake of beauty. But not all novelty in art is successful. Some slides over into the decadent and ugly. The Enlightenment rationality of the Minuet will slip over into Wagner, and from thence to jazz and rock'n'roll. Next thing you know you get Heavy Metal. I love the

Grateful Dead but I draw the line at Metalica. How is one to know where to draw the line?

There are no rules for how to break the rules safely, though *games* can be seen in this context as ways of limiting play to only those moves that are safe, moves that limit risks to contestants. The spread of human freedom means a spread of risk taking, and risks are not risks if they never fail. There will be failures, and there will be the need for means of insuring that failures are not too disastrous for too many people. Maybe we will never get a full insurance dividend, not unless we can avoid experiment on the scale of the USSR Experiments in new systems of social and economic organization should be smaller, and fail-safe mechanisms far beyond my imagination will need to be built in, checks and balances to rival the inventiveness of the Constitution. For, as I've said, the spread of human freedom means a spread of risk taking, and risks are not risks if they never fail.

This scenario is not utopian because evil will not have been eliminated. On the contrary, the close bond between freedom and transgression means that some confrontations with evil are virtually inevitable. Though it may sound as perverse as Freud's uncovering of infant sexuality, I see the origin of evil in the play of innocents, in the horsing around that got too rough, in the joke that went wrong. 'I didn't mean it that way,' he said. The Semiotic Turn can end in tears.

Watch the play of cute little kittens and you will see a rehearsal for the brutality of the tiger. See in the tussling of adorable little puppies the vicious attack of the wolf. But there is no viciousness or brutality in the animal kingdom, really. The moral overtones come only from minds that can add an interpretation of cruelty to what, in nature, is a mere act of survival. It takes a twisted mind to turn nature's metabolism into acts of evil. It takes a Semiotic Turn to add cruelty to nature.

It takes a twisted parent to convince a child that he is 'being mean' to his younger sister when all he was doing was playing. This move is called 'attribution' among psychologists. It's one of the ways that Mum and Dad can fuck you up. 'Don't pinch your sister,' is one thing. 'Don't be mean,' is another. By the latter I may learn not only how *not* to be mean, but also that, deep down, I *am* mean. Innocence disappears too quickly.

So the very thing that renders the sublimation of the economy possible – the Semiotic Turn – also renders transgression unto evil virtually inevitable. Earth might be fair, and almost all glad and wise, but human beings will not be angels, and evil will not be eradicated.

But human beings can be more truly human, more free, more creative, and less subject to the uniform necessities of nature. We have struggled up through the realm of necessity and now stand, more and more of us, on the brink of the realm of freedom. The shift to an information economy, the sublimation of the economy, is the crucial instrumentality for this transition.

Precisely because the very nature of information is to differentiate, precisely because information theory defines information as a difference that makes a difference – news, not noise or redundancy – an information economy can thrive only where mass-market conformity breaks up into highly differentiated niche markets, even into markets of one.

There was a fine match – a paradigmatic coherence – between industrial mass-manufacturing and the conformist values of the mass-market. If keeping up with the Joneses meant having the same car, and the genius of the industrial economy lay in producing lots and lots of the same car, then the match between supply and demand was, as it were, made in heaven. But this match is coming unglued with the transition from the industrial to the information economy. As Arnold Mitchell, creator of SRI's Values and Lifestyles program, used to put it, the Belongers (we used to capitalise the names of our lifestyle segments) liked to 'fit in,' but those who lead the new lifestyles 'prefer to stand out rather than fit in.' Individuation is the name of the game in the new economy. But individuation is (a) precisely what becoming more human is all about according to every wise psychologist from Jung to Eric Ericson, and (b) precisely what an information economy, as opposed to a mass-manufacturing industrial economy, is prepared to deliver.

The VALS program was all about charting the breakup of the mass market into segments or lifestyles that were not, strictly speaking, better or worse than one another, just different. But now the segments are shattering still further as individuals internalise the chaos of postmodern mores into the depths of their souls. There was a time when Achievers could be trusted to behave in all situations like Achievers, and Belongers would remain true blue Belongers, and the try-anything-once crowd, the segment we called Experientials, could be trusted to shop around. But now you see people who are Achievers by day and Experientials by night; ladies who shop at Bloomingdales one day and Price Club the next; men who wear black tie one night and a black motorcycle jacket the next. In short, people aren't staying true to type. A marketer's nightmare: people are becoming less predictable.

But this unpredictability should be cause for joy among humanists because it is precisely this unpredictability that we can just as well interpret as freedom flexing her muscles. The old shell of oppressive conformism is breaking. All that is solid melts into air? The constriction of Smalltown's norms for behaviour is being broken all over the globe and, one by one, individuals are emerging from the realm of necessity – what nature or nurture tells them they have to do – and they are stepping forth into the realm of freedom. And a new technology, a technology whose essence is to differentiate, will be there to greet them.

This is where we will get the advertising dividend. The old style of advertising depended on broadcasting, a one-to-many communication that blared the same message, over and over again, at everyone. Stage two was the stage of the partial breakup of the mass-market into segments. The first application of the information revolution to mass-manufacturing allowed for shorter production runs. Economies of scale could be chopped into smaller pieces that, still economically, could satisfy niche markets. Advertising was then customised to tailor the right message about the right product to the right segment through the right medium. This was called narrowcasting. Advertise McDonalds and pick-up trucks on Saturday afternoon network telecasts of the bowling championships. Save the BMW ads for the reruns of *Brideshead Revisited*.

We are still at a stage somewhere between broadcasting and narrowcasting, somewhere between an industrial and an information economy, somewhere between what I have arbitrarily labelled stage one and stage two. But a perfectly plausible scenario can be drawn for stages three and four. People, human beings, are pressing beyond mass conformity, and on beyond niche segmentation, to segments of one. Individuation. And information technology is capable of following them there. Computers are perfect for the task. *1984* was wrong in this respect. Assembling and recording lots of information about individuals need not mean Big Brother's invasion of your privacy. Instead it can mean the careful tailoring of the traffic of marketing information so that I receive information about all and only those things that my purchasing behaviour shows I'm interested in.

We already see the first signs of this transition, albeit in a form that any fool can see through, namely, the junk mail that shows up announcing that, yes, you James Ogilvy have been chosen . . . But this is just the first adolescence of information technology at work. Stage three follows broadcasting to the mass (stage one) and narrowcasting to the few (stage two) with communication to segments of one (stage three). The American Express bundles of one-page catalogs are subtler than the mailings from Publishers' Clearing House. Amex doesn't plaster your name all over everything. But your bundle is not the same as my bundle. Computers have seen to that.

Soon, I don't know how long it will be, I will no longer receive the Sears catalogue, or even the Smith & Hawken catalogue. I will receive the James Ogilvy catalogue. Stage four: narrow-catching (a word Stewart Brand came up with). This is what American Express is trying to give me. They just haven't got enough information about me yet. But when each of us can receive our own pesonalised catalogue, then we will be ready to distribute the advertising dividend. Then the offensive blare of persuasion will give way to the quieter hum of real information – differences that make a difference to individuated individuals. Then earth might be fairer when fewer billboards deface the countryside or the city skyline. It is possible. This is the direction in which information technology is taking us, and human freedom, I think, wants to go there.

Of course human freedom is very playful, even capricious. And as I've mentioned, in the play of innocents the seeds of evil and transgression are born. But as playwright and philosopher, Friedrich Schiller pointed out in his *Letters on the Aesthetic Education of Man,* 'Man is most truly human when he plays, and when he plays, most truly man.' In our playfulness we will keep remaking human life as we go along, better and better for the most part, but occasionally worse.

The fall into time will be more widely acknowledged. Imagine a world where people were able to swim in the tides of change rather than drown in confusion. Employers will be looking for swimmers, people who can keep up with time's current. They are the best at coping with change. In a scenario where most people were comfortable with a certain amount of change there would be less reactionary insistence on the sanctity of tradition, and less certainty about the justification for punishing transgressors.

The democratisation of meaning in this scenario will take the form of an evolutionary survival of the fittest interpretations of family life, romance, success. There will not be just one pattern of perfection toward which all would aspire in some recrudescence of industrial standardisation. Instead the paradigmatic preoccupation with difference over identity will encourage differentiation and experimentation, if not transgression. There will not be one best way of being human, but a rich ecology of species in the gardens of the sublime . . .

There is no clear *end* to this scenario just because embracing the fall into time means that there will be no finality, no goal which, once reached, would mark a conclusion. In this sense, too, this scenario is not utopian. I have not drawn a blueprint for an ideal society. Instead I have tried to reinterpret parts of the present – e.g. the information revolution – through the lenses of a paradigm shift already taking place in the human sciences. I believe that some of the phenomena that others lament – the decline of traditional orthodoxies, the melting into air of firm foundations – can be reinterpreted in ways that could contribute to a *better* future. But it is clear to me that this better future cannot be seen in terms of incremental improvements of the commonplace. A paradigm shift is required if we are to reinterpret the present as the prelude to a better future.

What we must do if we are to contribute to the story is not invent a new paradigm out of whole cloth. Rather, we need only look around and see what is already happening in the human sciences. There we find the Semiotic Turn already accomplished, a preoccupation with difference over identity already evident, the fall into time already acknowledged, and the democratisation of meaning well under way. What we must do is weave these threads into scenarios that have normative import, scenarios that carry the transition from explanation to narrativity further into a future we would like to leave to our grandchildren. Truly, Earth might be fair, and almost all glad and wise. We must just use our imaginations to spin out scenarios of better ways to play.

NOTES ON CONTRIBUTORS

Michel Andrieu is Deputy Head of the Advisory Unit to the Secretary-General of the Organisation for Economic Co-operation and Development (OECD) in Paris.

Kjell Dahle is a political scientist, but as a result of curiosity and addiction to odd combinations he also has exams in Bulgarian philology and theories of statistical probability. In fact, most of his time at the University of Oslo was spent within the student alliance 'Green Grass'.

After working in the Centre Party Youth Organization, he spent several years at the Norwegian Research Council for Science and the Humanities, and at the Alternative Future Project. He is active in the broad social movement 'The Future in Our Hands', but has also participated in more obscure activities like the 'Environmental Group of 13th October', blocking city traffic on several occasions.

He is now chief editor of the tiny Centre Press Agency in Oslo.

First educated in classics, **A. John Dakin**, urban planner, architect, and social scientist, has a major interest in psycho-cultural and social perspectives on our global ecological dilemma.

He has worked in England, France (with Le Corbusier), Switzerland, Africa, and Canada. Now Professor Emeritus of Urban and Regional Planning, University of Toronto, he has contributed academically to the development of futures studies and system theory in application to planning. His last book, *Feedback from Tomorrow*, brought together systemic approaches to global questions, certain technologies, and social-cultural perspectives. He hopes shortly to publish a new book dealing with our human dilemma in its psychic, social, and environmental dimensions.

Noriko Hama is an economist attached to Mitsubishi Research Institute, which she joined in 1975. She has been based in London since April 1990, where she acts as the company's chief representative as well as resident economist. Her main areas of expertise are in the fields of international finance and trade, and monetary issues in general. She has written and co-authored books on the United States, Japan and various currency-related topics. Her belief is that the hallmarks of a good economist are obstinacy, self-righteousness, and scepticism where the views of others are concerned, although these three elements alone without a flare for searching out the truth would simply tend to make one a very nasty person. She is confident that she has a large dose of the three elements, while the quest for truth will remain a life-long passion.

Willis Harman is President of the Institute of Noetic Sciences, a nonprofit research and educational organisation whose purpose is to expand knowledge of the nature and potentials of the mind, and apply that knowledge to the advancement of health and well being for humankind and the planet.

For sixteen years prior to that he was at SRI International where he initiated a futures research program to assist strategic planning and policy analysis for corporate and government organisations.

He is also emeritus Professor of Engineering Economic Systems at Stanford University, and a member of the Board of Regents of the University of California. In addition to BS degree in Electrical Engineering, and an MS degree in Physics he has a PhD in Electrical Engineering. He is also author of many texts on electrical and systems engineering, futures research, social policy and analysis and societal transformation.

His Royal Highness Crown Prince El Hassan Bin Talal, the youngest brother of His Majesty King Hussein and heir to the throne of the Hashemite Kingdom of Jordan, was born in Amman on the 20th of March 1947. He was educated in England and attained a B.A. (Hons.) in Oriental Studies from Christ Church College, Oxford in 1967.

He has played an outstanding role in the nation's life, sponsoring numerous initiatives, and acting as patron or chairman of a large number of organisations with national and international dimensions and significance. His activities and interests cover economic planning, geo-politics, education, science & technology development, bilateral and multilateral dialogue, Islamic civilisation, humanitarian issues and youth welfare.

While addressing the 36th session of the United Nations General Assembly in 1981, His Royal Highness proposed the establishment of a New International Humanitarian Order, resulting in the foundation in 1983 of the Independent Commission on International Humanitarian Issues, of which he was co-chairman. He is the author of three books, as well as numerous articles for leading international journals.

Vaclav Havel poet, playwright, human rights leader and now President of Czech and Slovak Federal Republic. He published his first play – the Garden Party – in 1963 and has received international acclaim for his work ever since. He was co-founder of the Charter '77 human rights movement, the Committee for the defence of the unjustly persecuted in 1978 and Civic Forum in 1989. Under the communist regime he spent many years in jail or under house arrest.

Francis Kinsman became a freelance business consultant, broadcaster, author and futurist in 1972, having spent 15 years in financial services in the City of London.

He specialises in the financial service sector, the impact of social change on business and management, corporate responsibility and general cultural and social trends – particularly of a greenish tinge. His clients include corporate, government and academic organisations.

He is also a compulsive networker having founded two such organisations – The City Liaison Group and the Business Network. He is also a qualified Counsellor, a Master of Arts and a Fellow of the Chartered Institute of Secretaries and Administrators, the Chartered Insurance Institute and the Findhorn Foundation.

Ervin Laszlo is Rector of The Vienna Academy for Global and Evolutionary Studies, principal advisor to the Director-General of Unesco, and founder and head of the General Evolution Research Group. He is the author or co-author of 50 books and over 300 papers and articles. A member of the Club of Rome, the World Academy of Arts and Science, the International Academy of Science, and editor of *World Futures: The Journal of General Evolution*, he has served as professor of philosophy, systems science and futures studies in various universities in the US, Europe and the Far East.

Wolfgang Michalski is Head of the Advisory Unit to the Secretary-General of the Organisation for Economic Co-operation and Development (OECD). In this capacity, he is also responsible for directing the OECD International Futures Programme.

He joined the OECD in 1976 as Deputy Director of the Interfutures Project. Prior to that, he was Chairman of the Board of Directors of the Institute for Technology and Economics (ITE) and Executive Vice-President of HWWA-Institute for Economic Research in Hamburg/Germany.

Wolfgang Michalski holds a professorship in Economics at the University of Hamburg. He has published 10 books and more than 50 papers on economic growth, structural adjustment and international trade policies.

Sheila Moorcroft is a self-confessed optimist. That, plus a highly developed sense of curiosity and love of 'what if?' enabled her to move from providing more conventional strategic planning research and consultancy, into futures research. She has now been active in the field for over a decade focusing on scanning techniques, issues identification and assessment and the implica-tions of social change and alternative scenario development. Before becoming a freelance consultant, she spent many years at SRI International and Applied Futures Ltd. Her research includes *The Future of the UK 2010, An Optimistic Scenario for Healthcare*, and *The Home of the Future*.

Robert Muller – a citizen of France he has devoted his career to peace and transcending national divisions. After completing a doctorate in law and economics he joined the UN in 1948 rising to the rank of Assistant Secretary General. During his time there he was one of the main architects of the UN institutional system in the economic and social fields, the main idea man and trusted collaborator to three Secretary Generals. He is now Chancellor of the University for Peace where he continues to write, teach and speak at conferences.

James Ogilvy is Managing Director of Global Business Network, which is headquartered in Emerville California. He is the author (with Paul Hawken and Peter Schwartz) of *Seven Tomorrows*. (Bantam 1990). Prior to co-founding GBN with Peter Schwartz in 1987, he spent seven years at SRI International (formerly Stanford Research Institute), and before that he spent over ten years teaching philosophy, mostly at Yale.

James Robertson is an independent writer and speaker. His latest book is *Future Wealth: A New Economics For The 21st Century*. Earlier books include *Future Work* and *The Sane Alternative*. With Alison Pritchard he edits *Turning Point 2000*. He was one of the founders of The Other Economic Summit (TOES) in 1984. From 1960 to 1963 he worked in the British Cabinet Office, and from 1968 to 1973 as director of interbank research in the City of London.

Philip Sadler read sociology at the London School of Economics. After an early career in the Civil Service he joined Ashridge Management College in 1964 as Director of Research, becoming Principal in 1969 and Chief Executive in 1988. Since 1990 he has been a freelance writer and consultant. He was awarded the CBE in 1986 and the honorary degree of Doctor of Science by City University in 1990. His writings include *Managerial Leadership in Post Industrial Society* (Gower 1988) and *Designing Organisations* (Mercury 1991).

Elisabet Sahtouris is an American biologist and philosopher who has been living on a Greek island for ten years. She is both a lecturer and author – her most recent book *Gaia: the journey from Chaos to Cosmos* was published in 1991. She is also co-founder of the World Wide Indigenous Network through which she pursues her interests in indigenous science and is currently compiling an anthology of native women's wisdom from around the world.

Ziauddin Sardar was born in northern Pakistan. At a tender age he moved with his parents to London where he grew up suspended in a number of cultures. An avid consumer of postmodern cultural products, he lives a multicultural life: changing identities – now 'Islamic', now 'Pakistani', now 'Western', now 'Radical' – and professions – now writer and journalist, now TV producer, now information scientist, now Muslim futurist – along with geographical locations.

He is the author of numerous articles, papers and reviews as well as seventeen books, including the highly acclaimed *The Future of Muslim Civilization and Islamic Futures: The Shape of Ideas to Come*. His most recent book is *Distorted Imagination: Lessons from the Rushdie Affair*. Currently he is engaged in writing a non-Western history of Western culture seen through the films of Arnold Schwarzenegger.

Malcolm Skilbeck is an Australian who has spent much of his life working as an educator in England, Northern Ireland, Australia and now France. During his career he has been a school teacher, adult education lecturer, university professor and Vice Chancellor, curriculum developer and adviser and consultant on national and international projects in education and training. His publications have been mainly in the fields of educational policy, school curriculum, teacher education and educational theory. His present position is Deputy Director for Education in the Paris-based Organisation for Economic Co-operation and Development. He is married with five children, by his present and former marriage. Apart from education his main interests are social and political theory, literature and gardens.

Rick Slaughter began his teaching career in the UK in the late 1960s. He holds a PhD on the role of futures studies in education and now lectures at the University of Melbourne where he is responsible for a Diploma in Education and two Masters courses. His major interests are in conceptualising the transition from industrialism, changing paradigms of knowledge, strategic planning, the study and implementation of foresight and the application of futures approaches in education. He is convenor of the Foresight Research Unit and a member of the editorial board of the journal *Futures*.

His publications include a curriculum guide *Futures Tools and Techniques* (1987) a monograph *Recovering the Future* (1989) an anthology *Studying the Future* (1989) and a resource pack *Futures Concepts and Powerful Ideas*. Current projects include a resource pack on Graffiti and a book The *Foresight Principle* (forthcoming from Adamantine Press).

James B. Smith lives with his wife, Karen, in Half Moon Bay, near San Francisco. He is a founding partner and director of the Business Futures Network, Ltd. (London) and has worked in the field of environmental scanning since 1976 at SRI International and the Global Business Network. Jim, a native Californian and self-described radical middle-of-the-roader, has a 31 year-old son, Steven, and a 20 month old daughter, Aileen.

Keith Suter is President, Centre for Peace and Conflict Studies, University of Sydney, and Consultant to the Conflict Resolution Network. From 1986 to 1990 he was the Director of the Trinity Peace Research Institute, Perth. He was previously the General Secretary of the Uniting Church's Commission on Social Responsibility, and Federal President of the United Nations Association of Australia. He is Chairman of the Australian Branch of World Federalists, a member of the Executive Committee of the International Law Association and a member of the Advisory Board, World Military and Social Expenditures, Washington DC. He was Chairperson of the 1984 Independent Inquiry into Nuclear Weapons and other Consequences of Australian Uranium Mining. Dr Suter is one of the twenty recipients of the Australian Government's Australian Peace Awards. He is author of several books and numerous articles, and is in popular demand as a lecturer.

W. Warren Wagar is a historian and futurist whose interest in things to come was first aroused at a tender age by reading the books of H.G. Wells. After taking his doctorate in European intellectual history, he taught history at Wellesley College and the University of New Mexico, and is now Distinguished Teaching Professor of History at the State University of New York, Binghamton. His first book, *H.G. Wells and the World State*, was published in 1961. Since then he has written or edited fourteen other books, including, most recently, *The Next Three Futures: Paradigms of Things to Come* (1991). He is a Vice President of the H.G. Wells Society. In his spare moments, he reads and writes science fiction. The second edition of his *A Short History of the Future* is to be published shortly.

Geoff Woodling is co-founder and partner of the Business Futures Network – a worldwide network for identifying and assessing the development of new and existing issues affecting business.

Having read geography at St Catherine's College Cambridge, he joined British Steel to plan for its expansion in the 1980s, after which he spent 8 years at Industrial Market Research concentrating on the future market potential for steel and transport technologies. Then, having spent 2 years on secondment to London Business School researching into innovation management, he became Director of SRI International's Business Intelligence Program in Europe where he founded the European Issues Group – the predecessor to Business Futures Network. In 1988, he moved on to Jones Laing Wooton where he developed the first international management consulting practice in the real estate industry, before setting up his own company in 1991.

WORKS MENTIONED
BY THE CONTRIBUTORS
IN PASSING

Adams, Gordon 1982: *The Iron Triangle: the Politics of Defence Contracting* (New Brunswick. New Jersey: Transaction)

Anon. 1991: *'The World's Top Superpower'* Pax et Libertas (Geneva)

Barasch, David and Judith Eve Lipton (eds) 1982: *Stop Nuclear War: A Handbook* (New York: Grove)

Barfield, Owen 1985: *Rediscovery of Meaning and other Essays* (Middletown, CT: Wesleyan University Press)

Benoit, Hubert 1959: *The Supreme Doctrine: Psychological Studies in Zen Thought* (New York: Viking)

Bergson, Henri 1974: *The Creative Mind: an Introduction to Metaphysics* (New York: Citadel Press)

Berman, Marshall 1981: *The Reenchantment of the World* (Hartford Conn: Cornell University Press.)

1982: *All that is Solid Melts to Air* (New York: Simon & Schuster)

Berry, Thomas 1988: *Dream of the Earth* (Sierra: Nations & National Philosophy Library)

Bookchin, Murray 1990: *Remaking Society: Pathways to a Greener Future* (Boston: South End Press)

Braudel, Fernand 1980: *On History* (Chicago: University of Chicago Press)

1982: *Structures of Everyday life* (New York: Harper and Row)

1983: *The Wheels of Commerce* (New York: Harper & Row)

1984: *The Perspective of the World: Fifteenth to Eighteenth Century* (New York: Harper & Row)

Busuttil, S. et al, (eds.) 1990: *Our Responsibilities to Future Generations* (Malta: Foundation for International Studies.)

Campbell, Joseph 1973: *Myths to Live by* (Auburn, CA: Condor Books)

1983: *Renewal Myth & Rights of the Primitive Hunters & Planters* (Dallas: Spring Publishing Group, US group)

Dahle, Kjell 1991: *On alternative ways of studying the future*. International institutions, an annotated bibliography and a Norwegian case. (Oslo: Alternativ Framtid.)

1991: *Participatory Futures Studies: Concepts and realities*. Paper presented at the World Futures Studies Federation World Conference in Barcelona.

Dammann, Rika 1979: *The future in our hands. What we all can do towards the shaping of a better world*. (Oxford: Pergamon)

de Jouvenel, Bertrand 1967: *The Art of Conjecture* (New York: Basic Books)

de Montaigne, Michel 1580: *Essais*

Drexler, Eric 1987: *Engines of Creation* (New York: Doubleday)

Fedigan, Linda M and Asquith, P J 1991: *The Monkeys of Azashiyama: Thirty Five Years of Research in Japan and the West* (Albany: State University of New York Press)

Fell, Barry 1978: *America BC* (New York: Pocket Books)

1980: *Saga America* (New York: Times Books)

Friberg, Mats 1986: *Deltagande framtidsstudier*. Om VETA-metodologien. (Participatory futures studies. The VETA methodology.) Appendix 7 to *Att studera framtiden*. (Stockholm: Statens offentliga utredningar)

Fromm, E. 1978: *To Have or to Be?* (London: Jonathan Cape.)

Galtung, Francis 1909: *Essays on Eugenics* (Eugenics Education Society)

Galtung, Johan 1971: *On Future Research and its role in the world*. In *Challenges from the future*. Report from the World Futures Studies Federation Second World Conference in Kyoto (Tokyo: Kodansha.)

Halsaa, Beatrice 1988: *A feminist utopia* (Oslo: Alternativ Framtid) Also published in Scandinavian Political Studies 4.

Harman, Willis 1990: *A Reexamination of the Metaphysical Foundations of Modern Science* (Sausolito: Institute of Noetic Sciences)

Hesse, H. 1951: *Siddhartha* (New York: New Directions.)

Hills, John (ed) 1990: *SEED of action: A report on the Bergen process and the SEED Popular Forum*. (Oslo: Alternativ Framtid)

Jaffe, Anita (ed) 1989: *Memories, Dreams, Reflections* by CJ Jung (New York: Viking)

James, William 1974: *Essays in Pragmatism* (New York: Free Press)

Jonas, Hans 1958: *The Gnostic Releigion: the Message of an Alien God and the Beginning of Christianity* (Boston: Beacon Press)

Jones, Steve 1991 (London: BBC Reith Lectures)

Jungk, Robert and Nobert Mullert 1989: *Futures Workshops*. (London: Institute for Social Inventions.)

Larkin, Philip 1974: *'This be the Verse'* in *High Windows* (London: Faber)

Lee, Peggy 1955: *Is that all there is?*

Lovelock, J E 1979: *A new Look at Life on Earth* (Oxford: Oxford University Press)

Gaia: A new Look at Life on Earth (Oxford: Oxford University Press)

Macy, J. 1991: *World as Lover, World as Self* (Berkeley, California: Parallax Press.)

Maslow, Abraham 1959: *Hierarchy of Needs* (New York: Harper & Row)

Milbrath, L. 1989: *Envisioning a Sustainable Society* (New York: SUNY Press.)

Milton, John *Paradise Lost*

Mitchell, Arnold 1975: *Values and Lifestyle Program* (Menlo Park: SRI International)

Ornauer, Helmut, Hakan Wiberg, Andrzej Sicinski, and Johan Galtung, (eds) 1976: *Images of the world in the year 2000.* A comparative 10 nation study. (Haag: Mouton.)

Sahtouris, E 1989: *Gaia: the Human Journey from Chaos to Cosmos* (New York: Simon & Schuster)

Salisbury, Harrison E 1983: *A Journey for our Times* (New York: Harper & Row)

Schindler, Craig and Gary Lapid 1989: *The Great Turning: Personal Peace and Global Victory* (Santa Fe, New Mexico: Bear)

Schumacher, E.F. 1977: *A Guide for the Perplexed* (London: Jonathan Cape.)

Shakespeare, William. *Julius Caesar*

Slaughter. Richard 1990: 'The Foresight Principle', *Futures* 22 (8) 801–819.

1991: *Futures Concepts and Powerful Ideas* (Melbourne: Futures Study Centre.)

'Changing images of futures in the 20th century.' In *Futures*, June 1991.

Snow, CP 1959: *Two Cultures* (Cambridge: Cambridge University Press)

Suzuki, David 1991: *Inventing the Future* (London: Adamantine Press)

Tough, A. 1992: *Crucial Questions About the Future* (London: Adamantine Press)

United Nations 1948: *Universal Declaration of Human Rights*

Watson, James D 1981: *The Double Helix* (London: Weidenfeld & Nicholson:)

Waugh, Evelyn 1945: *Brideshead Revisited*

Wilber, Charles K & Jameson Kenneth P 1983: *Confronting Reality* (Notre Dame, Illinois: University of Notre Dame Press.)

1990: *Beyond Reagonomics: A Further Inquiry into the Poverty of Economics* (Notre Dame, Illinois: University of Notre Dame Press)

Wordsworth, William 1850: Prelude. Book 11

INDEX